RUNNING TRACKS

RUNNING TRACKS

The playlist and places that
made me a runner

Rob Deering

unbound

First published in 2021

Unbound
Level 1, Devonshire House, One Mayfair Place, London W1J 8AJ
www.unbound.com

© Rob Deering, 2021

Text design by Ellipsis, Glasgow

A CIP record for this book is available from the British Library

ISBN 978-1-80018-044-4 (paperback)
ISBN 978-1-80018-045-1 (ebook)

Printed in Great Britain by CPI Group (UK)

1 3 5 7 9 8 6 4 2

CONTENTS

RUNNING, MUSIC AND ME

There's not much I like more than going for a run, out-side in the world, listening to some great tunes. I've always been inspired and fascinated by music, from my first adventures listening to my parents' vinyl albums and my older brother's cassettes as a little child, right through to the present day, where playing and enjoying music runs through my stand-up comedy like a stick of rock.

Running becoming part of my life has been more of a surprise.

A lot of people don't much like the idea of running. In fact, I think a reluctance to run is the predominant human condition, and has been for a long time. 'Oh no – I'm going to miss that bus!' or 'Oh no – I'm going to get eaten by that bear!' – it's an activity to be indulged in only in emergencies, and only for a brief amount of time; we plan to stop running as soon as we're on the bus, safe from the bear.

1

Even the keenest, most naturally adept runners must run through that moment, early on in a run, when their body says, 'So – we're doing this? We're not running from something, or after something? We're just . . . running?' That's the elusive sweet spot, the nirvana sought by those of us who run for pleasure: the mindful yet care-free place between stopping because, well, you want to, and stopping because you physically can't go on. That's the good stuff.

It took me a really long time to realise that this was a place I wanted to be – about thirty-five years, in fact. I was never one of those little kids who goes off like a rat out of a trap at every opportunity – I was far happier spending my waking hours reading or watching TV; for those things I had a voracious appetite. I also had a voracious appetite for food – and the physique you'd expect to result from such indulgence and inertia.

Once, when I was about eleven, I had an experience of running – or not running – that I remember well. I was at school, in west London. It was winter, a bitingly cold day, snow on the ground and beginning to fall again. Our PE lesson that week was 'cross-country'. This was not an attractive offer – there were no modern ideas of running to promote our physical and mental health; the whole concept was a somewhat Victorian exercise in suffering as a teaching tool. We were to run twice around Cranford Community School's extensive playing fields. I don't know how far that was – around three miles, I'm guessing – but our teacher, Mr Spong, might as well have asked me to run twice around the world, given how impossible this seemed to me. I ran until my throat was burning and I had a stitch – probably about fifty yards, maybe a hundred – and walked the rest, my knees freezing between my school-issue silky white shorts and blue-and-yellow football socks.

Towards the end of the second time around, about a hundred feet from the corner flag at the far edge of the most distant football pitch we were supposed to circumnavigate, I turned and cut across to the goal. A shortcut, yes, but a fairly humble one.

Mr Spong didn't see it that way. Frankly, I'd hoped he wouldn't see it at all, but he'd spotted my manoeuvre from whatever cosy little spot he was watching from, and he gave me a detention. A detention! I remember thinking how ridiculous the whole endeavour was; how far beyond my comfort zone I'd been expected to go – although I doubt I had the phrase 'comfort zone' to hand at the time. I knew that detention had no power to rehabilitate; that I, a pretty good student, would happily have taken that punishment over and over again in preference to the unimaginable nightmare of running twice around the playing fields.

But yesterday – a cold December day – I went out, of my own volition, and ran twice around the flat, muddy, football-field-filled space that is Hackney Marshes. I stuck close to the edges to be sure I got the full mileage – just over two miles a lap, four-point-two miles in all. I ran there and back, too – adding almost another five miles. A nine-mile run, mostly in the dark.

I loved it.

How did I get from there to here? It still bewilders me. But I keep thinking of my dad; I can see him in the kitchen, around that same time – the early eighties – in his dark-blue dressing gown with a cup of strong black coffee. 'Eugh,' I said – I was eleven, remember – 'I can't stand hot drinks; I don't think I'll ever like them, even when I'm a grown-up.' Easy-going but clear-sighted as ever, he said, 'You will. By the time you're my age' – he'd have been just over forty – 'you'll love black coffee.' And he was so right.

Over time I think I've become more and more like my dad – or at least realised I'm like him – and not just in the beverage department. I suppose I was always going to, but I think the trigger was becoming a dad myself; I just started emulating his example. My dad, Barney, loved music, books, TV and food and drink with the same passion that I do, a passion I would later recognise as unusually fervent. He wasn't a runner, but he was a great sportsman: an expert football player and cricketer. I am not, and have never been, a sportsman – cross-country was by no means the only discipline where I was

4

a disappointment to Mr Spong; such a brilliant name. But somehow, as the first phase of my life wrapped up and I settled into my adult existence – having a steady if ridiculous job, a home, a family – I began to access the same balance between living a happy, relaxed, mildly indulgent life and getting out several times a week for some fairly serious physical endeavour, that my dad had always had.

At the age of fifty-nine, Dad was diagnosed with Parkinson's. He was so sanguine; I honestly don't think I ever heard him say a negative word about it in the following, last eighteen years of his life, but it was a shame for someone so sporty to have to slowly lose control of their body in that way. I was still a few years away from taking up running then; I'd live through several more of life's traumas and bereavements – and, not incidentally, lose several stone in weight – before I set out on this road.

The biggest, most obvious influence Dad's condition had on my running life was to do with the charity Parkinson's UK. As you'll see in this book, my relationship with them has led to me running further – and further afield – than I could possibly have imagined when I started running 5k here and there in 2008, let alone when I trudged across the corner of that snowy football pitch in the early eighties.

But maybe his Parkinson's lit a spark in me: the realisation that, like being a husband and a father, drinking a cup of strong black coffee first thing in the morning,

HEADPHONES

Listening to music while you run is frowned upon in some circles.

This is strange, when you think of the people you see running out and about; so many of them have headphones on – or earbuds in – that the naked-eared purist would seem to be the exception. And modern running is totally tied in with twenty-first-century tech: those earbuds aren't just playing tunes or some great running podcast; chances are there's an app watching those runners from space and an additional voice in their ears telling them when to speed up or slow down, how far they've come and how much energy they're burning – even whether they've managed to escape a virtual horde of zombies, or been caught and eaten.

But if you sign up to a running event – a 10k, a half marathon, a marathon – headphone disapproval starts to creep in. Now, I totally accept that a warning against them may sometimes be appropriate. If you reduce your ability to hear when you're taking part in a group event, you have to make sure you can still make out instructions from marshals, sirens from emergency vehicles coming up behind you, etc. – and making participants aware of this is necessary.

But if you've never received one of these messages, you'd be amazed how often a passive-aggressive 'Do it without headphones anyway – so you can enjoy the day' creeps in. And occasionally the aggression isn't passive any more: 'This event is for proper runners, and if you're seen wearing headphones, you will be disqualified,' or words to that effect, really are spoken from time to time.

Well I'm not having it. If I get that second message, I'm either asking for my money back, or doing that run wearing my headphones, ready for a row. Yes, runners need to take care – but they do, so let's not lay it on too thick; I've never heard of some great running disaster where someone listening to Led Zeppelin missed an instruction and careened off a cliff. And if you can't get the attention of a marathon runner passing you at twenty-two miles, it's more likely to be because they're locked in a tunnel of pain and perseverance than because they've got Katy Perry on.

There's a traditional British idea of the cross-country runner – as seen, years ago, in comic strips about Alf Tupper or in the film *The Loneliness of the Long*

Distance Runner – that still very much abides. A working-class northerner in a vest, this man – it was always a man – would *not* listen to music, or anything else, while pounding miles and miles of chilly grey paths.

A modern version of this kind of runner is still very much a part of contemporary running – I know these guys; they're amazing runners and wonderful people. These days they're not just northerners, and some of them are women! Many of them are middle class, but, like comedians, they'd be unlikely to identify as such. Tech is embraced – but worn on the wrist. No phone. No headphones. The biggest philosophical shift is probably a culture-wide acceptance that running is good for you, physically and psychologically – it's no longer some kind of post-religious self-flagellation, offering self-worth only through great suffering. Punishing though it can be, we love it, it can help us love ourselves – and that's OK.

I have no problem with this model. In another universe I *am* that runner – we certainly share a level of obsession, and one of the most important things running brought to my life was leaving my phone – and all the texts, calls, emails, social networks and cat videos therein – at home for an hour. But I am also obsessed with music – and there is always a song playing in my head. When I listen to music, I'm not playing it into a kind of mental silence – there'll be a tune playing anyway; I'm merely taking control of what tune it is. That's not to say that I listen to music all day, every day – although I do pretty much listen to music all day, every day. If I'm writing a song – something I do fairly regularly for work – I'll let those melodies fill my noggin instead, and see where it goes.

But not when I'm running – because running is too rhythmic; it carries too much of its own music; I end up 'listening' to a mildly nightmarish, relentlessly repetitive tune I find playing in my skull as my feet hit the ground, my sleeve brushes my body, the breath goes in and out of my lungs. I have run 10k races without headphones a couple of times – one of those, I think, was because they weren't allowed, before I was such a zealous defender of my music – but I ended up literally attempting to play songs, whole albums, note for note in my head, just to keep my sanity and escape the step-step-step, breath-breath-breath mental hamster wheel.

Whatever works, eh? Anyone who runs is a runner, from someone doing the NHS's Couch to 5k for the first time – or trying to do it again – to some incredible, super-annuated fell runner who won't take their house key with them, never mind wear an Apple watch. But if you feel that, because I listen to music while I run, I'm in some way not accessing the entirety of the experience, the true majesty of running, that's where I need to put you straight. Music makes my running beautiful – not because of the great tunes, great tunes though they are, but because music damps down the mundane machinations of my mind. It helps me stop thinking about the act of running. It helps me stop thinking about my life before and after the run. It opens up a mindful, meditative space, and helps me be . . . present; alive to where I am; open to the wonderful world beyond this plodding machine. I honestly believe I'd be more likely to hear that marshal, or see that approaching meteor, with my headphones in.

So don't worry. It works for me. And I am a Proper Runner. We all are. Even though vests really chafe my pits.

1. NEW YEAR, NEW ME
Clissold Park 2008

In January 2008, when I was thirty-five years old, I made a New Year's resolution, as you do. More of a New Year's manifesto, actually. These were my new rules: no bread or pastry; no beer or wine or sugary soft drinks; no snacks; portion control.

One evening in the first few days of the year, I cooked a dinner my wife and I ate regularly at the time – but I made half as much as usual. There was plenty! We had a good bowlful each but no seconds. Previously, there would have been enough for us to have a whole second bowl each – except my wife, a sensible, healthy person, wouldn't. So I always had three bowlfuls: Daddy Bear's, Mummy Bear's *and* Baby Bear's porridge. Every time, lots and lots of times. What an eye-opener, to see so clearly how I'd been overeating this meal – spinach and feta garlicky risotto soup, in case you're wondering. And guess what? That wasn't the only meal I'd been overeating. Not by a long chalk.

I'd always been a big, round fellow. As an adult I'd tried to lose some weight and get fit a couple of times, with some success, but not for long, and only about once every ten years – in 1995 and 2004, in fact. In 2008, it stuck. I lost two stone in the first six weeks of the year, and by the summer I'd lost four or five – all without particular hardship. I choose my words carefully here – it was by no means an easy breeze; weight loss like that couldn't, and shouldn't, be. It was simply the right time for me. I had handily packed on some really unnecessary late-night-pizza weight in the autumn of 2007, and there were specific, long-term psychological reasons why this level of willpower became available to me that particular January. I bet you'd love to know what they were.

So, by summer that year I weighed the least I had as an adult – but don't worry; I wasn't by any means skin and bone. I'd just revealed an alternative, perfectly valid, full-sized me. Who knew! I certainly didn't, and it took some getting used to. They say keeping weight off is at least as difficult as getting it off in the first place, but I was in a slightly different place. The rules were conceived as an ongoing way to be healthy, not necessarily a weight-loss diet, so staying with them wasn't so hard. I could feel benefits: it was easier to go up stairs or to run for a train carrying several heavy bags – something I do so often I should maybe address tardiness in a New Year's manifesto another year. But there were also less welcome aspects of my new body I had to deal with: I felt the cold a lot more, and I'd dropped a shoe size, making the weird toe I've got on my right foot much more of a key player in the shoe-buying game. I bet you'd love to know what that looks like.

One day that summer, around the time my new weight had begun to level off, I carried my daughter home – she was coming up to two. I walked, holding her in front of me, without a baby-carrier, for five, ten minutes without difficulty – I realised, in that instance, she was a sentient, much more fun yet direct replacement for the gut I'd said goodbye to. I decided to go to a gym and test this new-found fitness. Once I'd put her down, of course.

People who knew me before I lost weight and got into running often assume that it was the other way round – that I got into running and lost weight as a result – but it wasn't like that. People looking to lose weight themselves are sometimes confused and a little bit miffed by this – I didn't go about it the way you're supposed to – but there it is. It wasn't at New Year, but six months later and four stone lighter, that I went to the gym for the very first time.

A nice woman showed me a bunch of machines, and I wandered about, having a go and trying to get comfortable with the idea. But it was ten minutes on the treadmill that would, as it turns out, change my life for ever: five minutes' fast walking, five minutes' gentle running, all with a slight gradient. I did it – I worked up a bit of a sweat, and I watched the clock desperately for the last minute, but I did it, and it wasn't so bad. I couldn't believe it. I still can't, on some level.

Not long after that, I was staying in Southampton for the weekend to do some shows, and I decided to try the gym there; there was one in the hotel – or rather there was one round the corner you could use if you were staying at the hotel. A pretty rubbish one, as it turned out. An old school gym – not 'old skool'; I mean like the gym in an old school – a wooden-floored hall with different coloured courts painted on it, a few lairy teens hooning around and not much else.

But there was a treadmill, and as you know I was now an expert, so on it I got. I did my ten minutes and felt fine – particularly as I was horribly hungover; without wine and beer, my Friday nights now tended to be fuelled by unwise amounts of gin and 'slimline' tonic – shudder. So I went round again . . . and again . . . and again. In the end, that Saturday I walked and ran for forty minutes. It wasn't pretty, but in those unpromising circumstances something brand new had begun.

A plan began to hatch. Running may not have been part of my New Year's resolution, but that September, as the new *academic* year began, I vowed to go out and run three times a week. I had established on those machines that I should be able to trot for around five kilometres, or three miles. Once I took this information outside, away from the clocks, counters and countdowns of a treadmill console – oh, the freedom! From that moment it would be years before I would run with even a phone in my pocket. So much easier to detach – to let go, meditatively speaking – out there in real life. I can't stand running on treadmills now, but I'm so grateful that those early ones showed me this so clearly; by the time I first ran outdoors, I already knew I could do this thing – now all I had to do was try to enjoy it, and the outside world was there to help.

It was a little like twenty years before, when I learned the basics of guitar-playing on a friend's shonky old acoustic. The strings were a huge, painful distance off the fretboard, but after weeks of suffering that pain and making that guitar work, I had a go on my brother's slim-necked, beautifully set-up Stratocaster: Wow, I thought, *this* is guitar-playing!

This was running.

It wasn't just the numbers on the machines that I rejected; I wanted no repetition or counting – no round and round the park for me. I came up with a nice route that connected two green spaces near me in north London – Highbury Fields and Clissold Park – looping them both but in a flowing, organic way, and just once each. I didn't take my phone, but I did have a tiny iPod Shuffle, a matchbox-sized clip full of lovingly chosen songs, that I attached to my shorts. You might think it was full of empowering lyrics and pumping beats, but no – I rejected those too. No on-the-nose lyrics. Some huge breakbeats and basslines, but nothing that would tune in too tightly with my natural running rhythm – that would remind me I was running! I know, I'm a dyed-in-the-wool contrarian, but I think I can explain this: I wasn't looking for inspiration; I was looking for distraction.

That first time I set out, I started running from my door and didn't stop again until I was home. It turns out I find that easier, mentally, than the walking/running/walking/running I'd been doing in gyms – but that didn't prevent from me taking it as a victory; I ran all the way, baby. It was beautiful in Highbury Fields – the very first signs of autumn were in the cool September air – and I kept running, continuing down through leafy streets back towards Stoke Newington's lovely Clissold Park. Around this point I must have headed into the longest sustained run of my adult life – probably my whole life up to that moment – but I didn't think of that; I was enjoying the weather, looking at the world, and listening to the music.

After about fifteen minutes I entered the park, following a woodchip trail under the trees along the edge of Green Lanes. I was listening to a song that even I can see is entirely counterintuitive at this joyful moment of physical exertion – 'Re: Stacks' by Bon Iver. It's a contemplative, heartbreaking song, the downbeat punchline to their seminal break-up album *For Emma, Forever Ago*. And it is stunningly beautiful. There are no big beats or pounding basslines – no drums or bass at all, in fact – and what little there is is *quiet*; guitar strummed so gently it can only be with fingertips, not a plectrum, Justin Vernon's falsetto singing not much more than a melodic whisper. As a running track there's pretty much nothing about it that fits the perceived profile, but that day it really hit the spot. Why? I suppose it's because it's all about letting go and moving on, which is what I was doing with my physical self, both in that moment and in life. Or maybe it's just a fantastic song that was benefitting from my full attention. Anyway, it took and held me completely for, what, two, three minutes? And when my reverie subsided . . . I was still running.

I can remember that moment so clearly: the sound of that sad, sad song, and my legs cruising over the woodchips below, as if they were nothing to do with me at all.

I ran twice more that week, three times the week after, and now, over twelve years later . . . I'm still running.

I'm still playing my brother's Stratocaster too.

Another tune like this: Another low-key heartbreaker, the polar opposite of what you'd expect a runner to listen to, but powerful enough to hold your attention while your legs and lungs do the work? How about Judee Sill's 'The Kiss'?

Another run like this: We're so lucky with our town and city parks in the UK, from the Town Moor in Newcastle to Preston Park in Brighton. Don't spoil them for yourself by running round and round them, though: loop one, then go down a couple of quiet streets to another, or the bank of a river or some such place – you're never far from water or greenery, wherever you might be.

2. THE QUAYS TO THE CITY
Manchester 2009

One of the ways running changed my life was almost entirely geographical.

As a jobbing club comedian, particularly in the first ten years of my career – also the first ten years of this century – my life revolved around weekend visits to UK cities. I got very used to heading out of my flat, and later my house, on a Thursday lunchtime and rolling back in some time on Sunday after three nights of performing one or two shows a night.

Sometimes I wouldn't be away at the weekend – I'd be working in London or doing one-night shows in places I could get home from – but other times I'd be away for longer, stringing together five, eight, ten nights of gigs around the country.

I visited a great slate of cities – Manchester, Southampton, Glasgow, Bristol, Brighton, Edinburgh, Bath, Leicester, Cardiff, Leeds, Nottingham, Newcastle, Birmingham and more – but it was a finite list; within a couple of years I'd been to all these places several times, and knew them well. Or, if I didn't know them well, I knew all the bits that suited me – good record shops, independent cinemas, places where you could get a good cocktail, not to mention where the Wagamama and the Sainsbury's Local were.

Sometimes I would fill the Friday and Saturday daytimes with work – I might have been writing an Edinburgh Fringe show, or exchanging long production emails, or sorting out money stuff. As the musical element of my set got more complicated, I'd often book a band-rehearsal room, just for myself. Back then, simply finding a good internet connection used to keep us travelling folk pretty busy. As Christmas approached – with more shows and longer stays away, as all the parties came to the clubs – I'd gleefully shop and wrap for days on end, arriving in, say, Birmingham as myself, and leaving laden with tempting-looking gifts like a mufti Santa.

I like some of these cities more than others, of course, but I kind of love them all, because for the time I'm there, I'm home. And back then, for all the writing, working and shopping, the daytimes ultimately featured a lot of time in cafés, cinemas and hotel rooms – all of which I'm good at. I know how I like my coffee. I know not to go to the cinema on Saturday afternoon, when the talkers will be there. And in my hotel, I don't moulder; when I arrive, I unpack – neatly; when I wake up, I get up, get dressed and make my bed.

But when I started running, I took my relationship with these places to the next level. Before I'd really done an outdoor run, I imagined the optimum version was down country lanes through the English countryside. Of course it wasn't; I'm a city boy, raised playing in the parks of west London and walking with my grandparents along the area's canal towpaths. Now that I was running, each of these other cities with which I was already friends opened up its loveliest outdoor spaces to me. OK, sometimes they weren't that lovely, or at least, not exactly Venice – but if, for example, you follow the Worcester and Birmingham Canal south from the heart of Birmingham, past the university and out towards the chocolate factory at Bournville, on a sunny morning, it is beautiful: water, wildlife, greenery, blue skies and fresh air; canal, railways and roads plaited together between exciting buildings full of academic potential and sweet treats.

Manchester was one of the first cities I used to tour to in this way; in the early 2000s I would go up on Tuesday to do a comedy night called XS Malarkey at Bar XS in Fallowfield, then stay right through till Sunday doing several nights at the often fairly rambunctious Frog &

22

Bucket. So, when I started getting booked for weekends at the city's mighty, legendary Comedy Store, I already knew where all the city-centre cinemas and the twenty-four-hour shops were. My new experiences began with nice hotels, but I almost immediately headed out behind them, along Manchester's superb waterways. Those stove-pipe-hatted Victorian businessmen may not have known how to respect the human rights of textile workers, but they sure could lay out a running route.

These days the Comedy Store put us comics up in a lovely place right by the old Haçienda nightclub, and I like to run out of town along the Bridgewater Canal to the big shiny excitements of Salford's MediaCity and back. When I first went up for the Comedy Store, they billeted us somewhere equally classy, just a couple of streets over, that backed on to what I thought was another canal but was actually the River Irwell, factored and engineered into the fabric of the city as it burgeoned in the nineteenth century. It, too, snakes out towards MediaCity, and this was my original Manchester running route. From late 2008, when I started running regularly, I had been finding completely new routes through these old, familiar spots; in spring 2009, I remember seeking out what was actually quite a sketchy riverside path and heading right past my hotel-room window on the opposite bank, literally thinking, 'Woah – who have I become?'

It was an inauspicious beginning for what would

become a favourite run in a favourite running city: it was raining, and there's a stretch of the river there that's a bit of a hinterland – redeveloped in the eighties, by the look of it, but perhaps forgotten a little as the tram flew over it to the newer museums, theatres and TV studios of Salford Quays. I ran along mossy pavements under old, moon-like street lights towards locked gates, gaps in the pavement opening up to show pipes and wires below . . . It was a 'this can't be right' route, and as it rained harder I had to give up the riverside and run across some scrubland to pick up a dirty little road that led to a dead end. Away from a dead end, in my case. Thank goodness for that little road, which was as handy for me as it would doubtless have been for, say, a couple of Mafiosi looking for a handy spot to lob a corpse into a shallow grave. Maybe that's what happened to the big and very dead bird I nearly tripped over.

Although there would have been witnesses. As I felt more and more of a Lycra-clad fool, trying to keep running as I scrambled up a bank in the middle of nowhere, brambles scratching at my legs, I looked up at a tram trundling past on the overhead line, full of Mancunians, doubtless on the way to work – it was first thing on a Friday – blankly staring back through the windows at me, like a jury. The verdict: idiot.

I kept running. The path by the river started up again, still sketchy and murder-friendly, but leafier. Then, close to Old Trafford, the path opened up into a wide pavement, the water now widening on my right towards new, silvery buildings and fancy bridges ahead. There were swans! And, in the distance, a person or two – looking more dog-walky than homicidal. MediaCity was more like the Emerald City for me that day. I ran through it, past the building where, a couple of years later, I would win *Celebrity Mastermind*, getting every one of my specialist-subject questions right.

Did I shoehorn that in?

On the return route, I found the good way; I crossed over Throstle Nest Bridge and came back along the towpath of the Bridgewater Canal, loving my run now – loving the whole thing, in spite of the dubious early stages. I chuckled as a ridiculously appropriate song came on in my headphones – the fantastic 'Thieves Like Us' by New Order. Expansive and filmic, I had fallen in love with it listening to their singles album *Substance* on cassette more than twenty years before. I remembered seeing shots of Manchester set to it on a *South Bank Show* episode about the band, before I'd ever visited the place. Now I was living it: as the chunky, mid-speed drum machine and the shimmery synths took their time building up to Peter Hook's enormous bass slide in the extended introduction, I was the video, striding through this fantastic city's history, from the twenty-first-century architectural adventure of MediaCity, through the quintessential

Victorian engineering of the bridges, tunnels and locks of Deansgate, towards the Haçienda, the iconic club this very band had helped to build – well, the car park where it used to be. As Bernard Sumner sang the deceptively glib, satisfyingly gnomic lyrics of love found and lost, I heard in them the story of my relationship with Manchester. I didn't know then how much I would fall in love with running there, but it all began on that rainy day. All that, plus I posted one of my earliest tweets later that morning – one of the first to be well received, anyway: 'Ah, a morning run along the banks of the Irwell. How nice to be— EWWW!!! DEAD GOOSE DEAD GOOSE!!!'

Another tune like this: 'Bizarre Love Triangle' – New Order at their most joyous, sounding as much like a blue sky as a bunch of machines can. The nearly-seven-minute mix for preference.

Another run like this: The Sheffield & Tinsley Canal, heading north-east from Sheffield, has a picturesque towpath and new things to see all the way to the M1 and beyond.

3. BACK TO NATURE
Wangford 2009

My wife's aunt and uncle are a pair of Scottish bohemians who live in Wangford, a little village in Suffolk. Their life is an idyllic blend of crosswords, cats, gardening and the arts, and periodically escaping to their cosy, Harry Potterish cottage there is a wonderful thing to be able to do.

Once, when our children were small, I dragged our little family to the Latitude Festival – a quarter of a mile away from Wangford – where I was doing some gigs. The weather wasn't great, my son was ill, and my daughter, although just big enough to walk, was small enough that the festival site felt about the size of a continent to her. The whole family festival trip was a bust. Halfway through the weekend we called it quits, struck camp and retreated to the village. There was something supernatural about the speed with which my wife's relatives had us in front of a roaring fire with a glass of red in one hand and a slab of Camembert in the other. Going to stay with Mo and Trapper is a wonderful thing.

So, once I was a runner, the first time we went to stay there held out great promise. Their village is three and a half miles from lovely Southwold, official coastal retreat for all north and east London *Guardian* readers. A few months into going out running three times a week, my regular distance was now seven miles. I planned to creep out before anyone else was up, cruise through the villages and fields to the sea and back, and return refreshed and ready for a full holiday schedule of cribbage and cheese-eating.

The streets were still and the sun was shining, and as I happily headed off, the church bell sounded a ding for quarter to seven. Up and out in fifteen minutes! I was convinced I could train my body to get used to this kind of schedule, so I breezily ignored the oh-please-God-no resistance it offered me at every step. Soon I'd be warmed up and enjoying the beautiful countryside, I told myself. I left the last houses behind and turned onto the lane to Southwold. Though still not a big road, it's a key connection and there was a fairly steady flow of traffic. I tucked myself into the right-hand side – there was no pavement – and when a car came towards me I stepped off, into the long grass, and tried to get myself as far out of the road and into the hedgerow as possible. This happened fairly often. I got stung by a nettle – ah, well. At least, I hoped, I wasn't in the way of vehicles coming from behind me – although I nearly had kittens when the bus came zooming past my left shoulder. I began to dread the moment when it would return – would the hedgerow have room for me when the village-hopper bore down on me from the front? Stress!

I was listening to music, of course. The songs were good; I'd been building up my playlist with classics from my youth. I had a very summery slice of the Cure, for example – 'Just Like Heaven' – as I trotted along by a golden field. I kept an ear out for cars – and buses – though. The field spread into the distance on my right, with a couple of those statuesque trees the farmer has to work round way out in the middle of it. More venerable trees lined the lane I was on, evenly on both sides; it must be an ancient and fairly important route, I thought. Another song played. The camber of the road started to make my knees ache; I was, by necessity, running on an unrelenting sideways slope. I daydreamed about running in the middle, on the white line, then pictured myself as flat and forgotten as the run-over – and then repeatedly run-over – ex-pheasants I saw there. I'd stick to my dusty edge. Another song. The golden field still spread out on my right, the avenue of trees in front – come *on!* The countryside is massive. I felt like I was running on the spot; it was like being back on a treadmill. A treadmill with a gorgeous view, yes, but also a painfully wonky treadmill, dusted with a light but constant risk of death.

After a while – a far longer while than my London-trained ADHD running brain was ready for – I reached a hamlet, where a stretch of pavement started up and took me past another church, a pretty building covered with Suffolk flint.

It took me past it for ages.

Another, mercifully shorter, stretch of car-dodging and hedge-dipping brought me to a bigger village, Reydon, with houses, a school, sports fields, all the gear – and flat pavement throughout. It was heavenly after the open country. As it turns out, I do like things a bit urban.

But now a new problem arose. My digestive system, adamant just half an hour before that it had no pressing needs, had a change of heart. Things escalated quickly. In the space of a quarter of a mile, I went from feeling tickety-boo to when-I-get-back-I-might-need-a-bathroom to I NEED A VERY SECLUDED HEDGE RIGHT NOW. I was desperate, trying to reframe my prudish brain into thinking of this whole thing in a more Bear Grylls-esque way – *Be cool, Rob. Squat down. Run on.* It was not me.

One glimmer of hope presented itself – Reydon's hotel, The Randolph. Would it be open yet? It was about twenty past seven, so the answer was: unlikely, but I was all in. I had no other plan.

The front door was locked. *AAAAGH!* But wait . . . a

young man with a hoover passed by inside. I tapped, and he let me in. I held it together to ask politely and without haste whether I might, perchance, pop to the bathroom, but I'm pretty sure the circumstances, and the beads of cold sweat on my brow, told him the whole sorry story. At least – thanks to him and The Randolph's facilities – it was now a sorry story with a happy ending; a transcendentally happy ending for a moment there. The relief! You can keep your forest, Bear Grylls – give me a just-cleaned hotel any day of the week.

I ran on into Southwold lighter, happier, freer – but the run still seemed to be rolling on into infinity, so, without reaching the sea, I admitted defeat and turned back for home. Like all there-and-back runs – as I was yet to learn – it didn't seem nearly such a distance on the return trip. Also, I didn't have to stop at the hotel, although just looking at the building gave me a glorious feeling of comfort and relief. But I had learned a couple of long-lasting lessons. The first was that my romantic, slightly crass idea of country running was a bit off. In time, I would experience some absolutely incredible trail runs, but I had definitely been underestimating the city. The second was that henceforth I would drink a couple of cups of coffee, give it half an hour and be sure that *all was right with the world* before trotting off into the middle of nowhere.

Once out of Reydon, past the little church and nearly back at the Wangford turn-off, I saw a baby rabbit lying in the road, apparently undamaged, like it was sleeping. It was heartbreaking and I had a little cry, but then I couldn't help but chuckle at my city uselessness. Dead animals, bowel movements, stinging nettles – poor little flower ... Truly, this was nature, red in tooth and claw.

The song that was playing at this point was Talking Heads' 'Once in a Lifetime'. The post-punk New York funk of golden-era Talking Heads is all fantastic music for running – rhythmic, relentless and lyrically mind-bending – and 'Once in a Lifetime' is the best of the lot, its mid-speed, upbeat, repetitive groove underpinning David Byrne's crazy hymn to modern American detachment. As I listened, in my own repetitive, steady jogging groove, I stumbled on some Suffolk-based detachment; I found myself in a country lane and I thought to myself, *Well – how did I get here?*

Running. You've just got to loosen up and let it in. In trying to live up to some half-baked idea of what I should be doing, what a run ought to be, I had come up against myself over and over again. I had to let it go. But running abides; my morning had still been brilliant and beautiful – just a bit more ridiculous than I'd expected.

I got back to the cottage, where Trapper somehow served me up poached eggs and fresh-baked bread before I'd started undoing my laces.

Another tune like this: So many funky, arty, New York-y seventies-into-the-early-eighties classics turn out to be great to run to – it really is a rich vein. Take David Bowie from that era, for example – 'Fame', 'Heroes', 'Sound and Vision', right through to 'Fashion'. Style for your mind, great grooves for your stomping feet.

Another run like this: Years after my first run in Southwold, I ran there again – this time north from the pier, along the beach, and back. It was still big-scale, relentless running, and the beach was tough underfoot with a challenging sideways camber – but this time I got it and loved it. And there were no toilet breaks, or buses.

4. SOFT, STRONG AND VERY, VERY LONG

Hong Kong 2010

I have a theory about treadmills. I think that to run steadily and safely on one, and not, say, go flying off the back onto the gym floor like that guy I once saw in a big, posh hotel – the guy running *in his jeans* – your subconscious has to be constantly alert, maintaining a kind of secret safety sub-routine.

This quiet awareness impairs other brain function, particularly meditative, right-brain stuff. Because of this, that earthbound feeling of running on a machine comes, I think, not just from boredom from looking at the same dull view for half an hour – though that is of course a factor; it's because one's ability to mentally unlock and drift into imaginative space is impeded. And if you're the kind of ascetic runner who can achieve a mindful-yet-unthinking equilibrium just in the rhythm of your breathing and your steps, maybe a treadmill offers an experience closer to 'the real thing' than is available to me.

My friend Susie Chan is an incredible endurance runner who has completed some of the world's toughest ultramarathons, and other extreme running events, like a twenty-four-hour run on a 400-metre track. The kind of runner who can achieve that kind of thing is the kind of person that I feel could transcend the mental drudgery of a treadmill and get into an appropriate running headspace – and, sure enough, Susie once broke the world record for running on a machine for twelve hours, clocking up sixty-eight and a half miles. She didn't enjoy it much, mind.

For someone who bitches about them so much, I've done my time on running machines. When I tour to cities in hot countries, even if I can get out and run outside now and again, I tend to use hotel gyms to keep up my mileage – particularly if I'm training for something. With all the excitement and challenge of new time zones, big gigs for international crowds and – let's be honest – stupendous buffets, I find myself more committed to my self-imposed training schedules than ever, squeezing in my trots no matter how awkward the timing or the environment, so as to keep some rhythm, sense and health in my life.

So I've actually run on machines with quite interesting views. When there used to be a Comedy Store in Mumbai,

I went there and ran in a gym that looked out onto a beautiful pool surrounded by palm trees and rare birds, then two buildings under construction, and beyond that to busy, busy streets all the way to the sea – a scene of constant activity. Plus, I had the extra distractions provided by the man who kept coming to ask me if I needed anything, and the microbe which required me to run back to my own bathroom every twenty minutes or so throughout my stay.

And, of course, I have my trusty headphones. Over time, in gyms, I have experimented with watching films instead of listening to music, to try to stop myself constantly watching the numbers going up on the console. And these things all help – as does music – but it was as I was watching a film while running that I came up with my theory. I found that, in a gym, I have to manually, actively, repeatedly make the decision to keep watching the film, or look at what's going on out of the window, or listen to the song. If I don't make the effort to shoulder open the doors of my own imagination, I'm just thinking treadmill, treadmill, treadmill, treadmill; whencanIstop, whencanIstop, whencanIstop, whencanIstop. When I'm running outside, I never have to decide to listen to a song – or to look at the world; I just ... do. And I never want to stop; the thought wouldn't cross my mind until I got to the point where I physically couldn't go on. And yes, I've been there – the New York City Marathon, that hangover I had in Birmingham ... but that's different.

I was developing this theory way back in summer 2010, though I didn't know it at the time. I hadn't been running all that long and I'd just signed up for my first half marathon, in the autumn, and – assuming that wouldn't break me – a marathon in the spring. So the events were months away, but they didn't half loom, and when I was lucky enough to go on tour to Hong Kong and Thailand, there was no way I was going to let my weekly mileage slacken off.

I went for a run outside in Hong Kong, and it was fantastic – as a cultural experience. I saw amazing things, particularly in the park: it was so full of people and stuff – nothing like the green spaces of London; round every concrete corner there was a new group of people doing an activity together, from cross-training to playing the *guzheng* – an ancient Chinese zither – and everything from Eastern and Western culture in between. I'll never forget it – but as a run it was a failure. I was stopping and starting and turning back all the time, and it was so hot. I wasn't so much drenched in sweat as entirely made of the stuff. They say we are 70 per cent water – I expelled it all that morning.

So my next run was going to have to be in the gym, and I was afraid. Afraid I didn't have the gumption to stay on a machine, running on the spot, looking at a wall, for the fifty minutes I'd decided were necessary. Then I had a brainwave: I would make a playlist of the longest songs in my laptop's library to help me through. If I only had to listen to – what? Six songs? Fewer? – that would make my run seem pretty short . . . wouldn't it?

It kind of worked. I think it was due to this as-yet-undiagnosed need to actively listen, to deliberately keep my attention on the music, that this playlist worked well. But it was a lot more like going to a lecture about listening to these songs than the imaginary gig – or rave – my subconscious usually goes to during a run. *Hmmm. I hear the guitar figure, and there's the bass coming in. Now I'll pay attention to the lyrics in this next verse.* That's the kind of thing that was going on in my head, and it was dry but it worked. I wasn't dry, though; despite the air-conditioning, I was still sweating fit to beat the band.

There were a fair few groups and artists on that play-list – I'm no stranger to prog rock, or remixes, or classical symphonies for that matter – but the stars of the day were, predictably, Pink Floyd. Within the space of their long-form noodling, I couldn't help but find some psyche-delic headroom, despite the limitations of the situation. After all, they may not be all about the repetitive beats, but this is still music originally designed for people in clubs to lose themselves along to. The band's extended solos are much more groove-based than those of later-established, rockier bands, the repetition of simple, chunky beats and basslines from Nick Mason and Roger

Waters as important as the long notes David Gilmour and Richard Wright layer over the top – with those sequences often balanced by sections fashioned of pure sound – bleeps, samples, swooshes and burbles. And throughout all this they really – *really* – take their time.

That day in Hong Kong, they soundtracked pretty much half my run with their song 'Echoes'. I wasn't that familiar with it – I cut my teeth on their mid-seventies duo of *The Dark Side of the Moon* and *Wish You Were Here*, getting into those two in reverse order. It all began one night – or early morning – in the late eighties. Hearing the crystal clarity of Gilmour's four-note riff in 'Shine On You Crazy Diamond' come ringing back in towards the end of the *Wish You Were Here* album after half an hour of other songs – and in my case after a long night of excess at a cooler-than-me friend's house – was a mind-blowing musical moment in my life. In that moment, all the prejudices I had about seventies rock dinosaurs and guitar solos disappeared in a – literal – puff of smoke, and I was in. Although I hid my copy of *Wish You Were Here* from my big, angry brother for years; as a post-punk purist, he would not have approved.

On the treadmill in the hotel gym in Honkers, I listened carefully and heard the blueprint for both those albums being laid out in the earlier 'Echoes'; in particular, the genius of the submarine-radar 'ping' that starts the track reappearing a full fifteen minutes later, followed by new, clean, crystal-clear chordal riffs that lead you back to the final verse. In amongst all the long, spooky noise of the middle section, we'd forgotten that this is, after all, a *song*!

On most days, and most of their tunes, Pink Floyd don't provide quintessential running music. Yet, in a way, they've got it down. Sweeping harmonies, chords and melodies for your head, mechanical riffs and circular rhythms for your feet – all in epic songs that get so far from where they start that by the time they bring the song back together, you know it anew. Not so much sounds *for* a long run as the sound *of* a long run.

I wouldn't listen to 'Echoes' on a run today – it's a tad too slow and spacious – but I often listen to 'Sheep' from *Animals*. Just a sprightly ten-minuter, the grooves are pacy but it's got the full break-right-down-and-build-it-back-up in the middle – including the return of the crazy noise you last heard two songs ago if you've been listening to the whole album; I love that trick. Plus the final, descending buzz-saw guitar chords are positively triumphant. I'm glad I listened to 'Echoes' when I did though; partly thanks to Pink Floyd, I did make it to fifty minutes on that treadmill in 2010.

I didn't enjoy it much, mind.

Before I left Hong Kong, I went out again. I took the Star Ferry across the water from Kowloon to the main island, then followed an incredible inside–outside route which climbed up alleys and escalators, then up and up under tropical trees, looking back to the skyscrapers now below me and picking up a high-level terraced walk that looped through a place called Aberdeen Country Park to the Peak, a viewpoint where you can suddenly see the ocean and more islands on the far side of the hill. It was one of the grand sights of my life; I'd love to see it again sometime.

Of course, that day I walked – and took the tram back down.

Another tune like this: 'Timeless', the twenty-minute opener from Goldie's album of the same name, remixes and blends all his early singles into one mega track, and although it's drum and bass rather than rock, it offers a similar journey to a long Pink Floyd song – detailed, epic and psychedelic.

Another run like this: If the city you're in is hot and busy, it's going to have to be a treadmill but, if possible, outside is always best. So, my tip is go somewhere cold. It was literally freezing when I ran in Estonia's capital city, Tallinn, and my shorts earned me some very quizzical looks, but it was a classic run I'll never forget.

5. LIFE LESSONS NEAR LANCASTER GATE

Hyde Park 2010

A friend of mine pointed out recently that the reputation of half marathons is lessened by their diminutive name; the maximum you can achieve is 50 per cent of a marathon – 50 per cent of something bigger, better and more widely recognised as a life goal.

This does not give half marathons their due. Thirteen-point-one – point-one! – miles is a really challenging distance, partly for the very reason that it's sort of doable. If you commit to running a marathon, or even further, people will expect you to train hard, for months, and if, during the event, you flag, cry, bleed or wobble, they'll say, 'Fair dos – this *is* a marathon.' Half marathons are perceived more like any old run, only with a bib on.

But they're further than that. If you're a regular runner,

maybe you usually get out and run five, six, seven miles. You might know it when you've done ten, but that's still just a long run. Somewhere between ten and thirteen – point-one! – things change. Somewhere around an hour and a half or so of solid running, your body runs out of fuel, and suddenly it's all about just hanging on in there.

So speaks the voice of experience. When I toddled down to Hyde Park on a crisp, sunny October morning in 2010, two years after I'd started running, I had no idea about any of this stuff. I just had a pair of trainers, a pair of headphones and a constant, joyous sense of surprise that running was something I could, and did, do now.

I'd signed up to run the Royal Parks Half Marathon for Parkinson's UK, and if it went all right, I'd do the London Marathon for them the following April. I didn't do this because I wanted to complete the endeavour – I did it to give something back. I'd fallen in love with running, and doing it for charity meant all those hours spent pounding pavements listening to my favourite music weren't purely self-indulgent. Plus, as a comedian, I had a fundraising platform that isn't available to some other runners. I already had a relationship with Parkinson's UK before I got into running, from doing charity editions of TV quizzes – now we've worked together for the best part of two decades, creating a Deering-shaped fusion of comedy, quizzing, running and fundraising that suits me down to the ground, and, I hope, works for them too – but that autumn was when running was first introduced to the mix. My dad, Barney, had Parkinson's, so he's the ultimate inspiration here – not just because he lived with the condition, but because when he was first diagnosed – as an otherwise fit guy in his fifties – he started working with the charity almost immediately. As a skilled business administrator, he really shook up those ageing volunteers in his local branch. 'Shook up' is perhaps an inappropriate choice of words.

So, in 2010, Parkinson's UK were happy to get me a place on that start line in Hyde Park; all I had to do was get round.

I hadn't done any specific training, but I was running seven miles three times a week. Did I ever run, say, ten miles in preparation? A sensible intermediate step up to the distance, with the added psychological breakthrough of running into double figures? I don't believe I did – but I should have done. However, I had three advantages: one, my naivety; two, the fact that I tended to always run at a very race-ish pace – although I wasn't really aware of this . . . see one; and three, that those three runs a week were just about enough training to get me round.

My disadvantages were, in essence, the same things. And a dreadful pair of shorts.

As I waited in the starting funnel, Sir Steve Redgrave got on the mic to say a few encouraging words and threw in the fact that, after a few miles of Westminster roads, the course re-entered the park. 'Careful,' he counselled. 'It's going to feel like you're nearly done, but you'll actually be less than half way round.' This was incredibly useful advice to catch in chit-chat seconds before the event – hearing that was a piece of luck for this newbie, and no mistake.

I was in such a good mood. Despite my reliance on my headphones, then as now, I wanted to show willing; to be a part of this huge group of people who'd come together to do the same, lovely thing. As we set off, running out of Hyde Park, past Admiralty Arch and on to Birdcage Walk, where the London Marathon ends, I popped my earbuds out and smiled at the people all around me. I wanted to make a few friends – maybe with that guy in the 'Vegan Runners' vest running barefoot – imagine that! But on taking them out I realised immediately – obviously – that this was not a party; everyone I could see was facing away from me. I chuckled; there was no music, no talk, not even traffic noise, as we ran a thousand-person hairpin turn on a closed Westminster Bridge. All I could hear was lightly effortful breathing, and the *pleh, pleh, pleh* of 2,000 trainers – plus the pit-pat of my plant-based friend's feet, naturally.

It was an eye-opener. *It's not a dinner party, Rob, or a music festival.* Every person there was busy running – on their own. What I comprehend now – did I then? – is that we were all together, just in a different way – a pure way, like an army, or a flock of birds. Anyway, lesson learned, I put my headphones back in and have rarely taken them out on a run since.

The Houses of Parliament, Embankment, the London Eye ... the Royal Parks Half immediately gives you London's sexiest wonders; the London Marathon makes you wait twenty-five miles for them. And the Royal Parks Half throws in Nelson's Column for good measure; that's not on the London Marathon route at all. Then, before you know it, you're back in Hyde Park, running alongside the sparkling Serpentine – although due to my, er, detailed research, I knew this didn't mean we were nearly finished; we were just about halfway. Thanks, Sir Steve.

The course in Hyde Park twists, turns, and switches back and forth – that place is enormous. It does mean that I saw my family – my wife and then-tiny children, and my mum and Parkinson's-y dad – twice. Though this was partly thanks to the shape of the course – they didn't have to walk far to reach another bend which was a mile or two further on for me – this was still a feat of family logistics from that crew that trumped anything I achieved that day. Unfortunately for them, their second 'There's Daddy' moment coincided with a weird spot of bouncy, slightly slippery, temporary plastic path – over a muddy patch, perhaps – so all they got at that point was an unending flow of runners, me included, going 'Woah', 'Easy', 'Watch out', 'Yikes', 'Woah', 'Easy' . . . etc.

It was all so new and exciting to me, I got a long, long way without actually considering the task at hand. I cruised along the long north edge of the park, travelling west next to the Bayswater Road, slightly downhill, passing the ten-mile mark with glee, and zigged and zagged again before I noticed anything unusual or difficult going on.

Between miles ten and eleven, out in the middle of the park, volunteers at a table were handing out Percy Pig sweets, and I couldn't understand it. I thought, *They must be expecting a bunch of kids to turn up.* Just a hundred metres or so later I thought, *Wow – I feel as if I'm running on empty. What I wouldn't give for a little energy-giving blast of sugar right now . . .*

Ah, I see.

But it was too late. Running on empty it would have to be. The vegan guy must also have done without; in those days, Percy Pigs were made with real pig. The only energy-giving fuel to get me through this last mile or two was going to be administered through my ears.

Musically, my luck was in. As I felt this abrupt physical fade, a squeal of feedback heralded the coming of a riff, a guitar riff so powerful and rocky, yet fluid and ornate, that it immediately distracted me completely. Then, as the muscular bass and drums arrived, I put my foot down and started – despite my tiredness – to overtake people, one by one, targeting them and picking them off coldly and efficiently.

The song was Muse's 'Plug In Baby', and I can't imagine a tune that, in that moment, could have served me better. A short, bitter blast of screaming yet pared-down rock, sharper and sourer than a Percy Pig but at least as strong. That riff! An Escheresque spiral staircase of angry sound climbing endlessly to nowhere, its ascending arpeggios woven over three chords, not four, so subconsciously your ear is never going to find that top step, but keep climbing forever.

By the time, just three minutes later, the final chorus dropped abruptly back to that riff one last time, Matt Bellamy's sky-high vocal soaring unsupported above it, I was through my unexpected running emergency – and the eleven-mile mark – still overtaking, feeling the finish line ahead.

Twelve miles. I'd never run this far before.

A last left put me on South Carriage Drive, the broad boulevard across the Knightsbridge side of the park; I was going slightly uphill now, but being pulled towards the climax of the run by a far friendlier song than 'Plug In Baby' – also a far sexier song, but that's a musical story for another time. I passed the impressive edifice that is the Albert Memorial without slowing down, reached the finish line, and got my first medal – plus a free banana.

What a moment! I felt really special – but not too exhausted to enjoy it. Hey – it was only a *half* marathon. At the back of my mind, I thought, *I must stretch*, but all the family were there, the park was resplendent in the sunshine, there was a post-run food festival . . . We had a bite, and then, while the kids had a splash in the Diana Memorial Fountain, I forgot stretching and made do with dipping my well-used feet in its therapeutically chilly waters.

Four days later, I was late for my train up to Edinburgh for a weekend of gigs. I ran into Euston station through pouring rain in a kind of Groucho Marx crouch, lugging my guitar, pedals and luggage. I made it, but as I took my seat I started to feel very odd indeed, as if my body was going into some kind of shock. I'm no doctor, but it seemed to be sending me a message, something along the lines of: 'For goodness' sake, leave me be.'

When I got off the train four hours later, I could barely walk. My left knee and hip were in terrible pain, and I spent three days roaring in clammy, ashen-faced agony, just about pulling myself together for my twenty-five-minute set each night and spending the rest of the time in a lonely tunnel of suffering.

Do your stretches, kids!

Another tune like this: Placebo's 'Nancy Boy' is an equally powerful use of the building blocks of rock, with a sixteen-beat rhythm that makes it fast and slow at the same time.

Another run like this: Speaking plainly, the Great North Run isn't quite as picturesque as the Royal Parks Half Marathon – the city of Newcastle-upon-Tyne at the beginning and the North Sea at the end are gorgeous, but there's a lot of dual carriageway in between. However, it's a great event; the atmosphere is second to none – it's like Christmas Day.

6. THE GADGET SHOW
Cyprus 2012

For me, one of the earliest, most First-World-Problem casualties of the 2020 coronavirus lockdown was the Limassol Half Marathon. My friend and fellow comedian/runner Paul Tonkinson and I – 'influencers' because of Running Commentary, the podcast we record together – had been invited to Cyprus to run it. The organisers were going to fly us out and put us up; they were really nice, repeatedly saying they didn't need anything from us in return. Literally, all they wanted was for us to come out, go for a run in the sunshine and enjoy ourselves. It was one of those lovely things that rarely happen. And, in this case, didn't.

So, a sweet jolly for sure, but for me – for both of us, actually – it would also have been a nostalgic pilgrimage.

A little while back, I used to go to Cyprus for a week a couple of times a year to entertain people from the

Armed Forces going through 'decompression' – a brief stopover for them on the journey back to the UK from whichever war zone they'd been stationed in, where they'd do a few relaxing, normal things to ease the gear change from conflict to life at home.

It was a wonderful thing to get booked for – sunshine and time away in a villa justified by this fun, worthwhile work – and even more inspiring for me because the shows were a blend of comedy and music, so along with my regular social life of being away with comedians, I was hanging out and jamming with musicians.

And then there was the running.

We'd stay in a pair of villas between the hillside village of Pissouri and Pissouri Beach below. It was a Grand-Old-Duke-of-York kind of place, neither up nor down, and when I ran up, I ran up, and when I ran down, I ran down, and when I was only half way up, I was . . . back at the villa.

I hadn't been running all that long when I first went, and I'd never run up any hills to speak of. I figured that I'd start by going up, while I was fresh, and then I'd have coming back down in hand. So, I set off running uphill, towards the village. Very soon, I saw a dead snake at the side of the road. Yikes! Must have been there for ages, right? No snakes in January, even in Cyprus . . . right? Anyway, this one was dead, and on I went. I was pleased to find that, by slowing down to an appropriate pace, I could do this – and keep on doing it. When I reached the village, I kept on through, following the slope in front of me up to the ridge, only turning left to go downhill once I'd reached the top. It was a gentle downhill, keeping me on the high ground for some distance – I didn't want to squander the elevation I'd gained straight away. I absolutely love the feeling of finishing a climb but carrying on running; the feeling that you're getting a break and recovering, even as your legs and lungs keep on keeping on. It's a great shortcut to that primal sense that I think runners are looking for: that running – forwards, not fast or slow, no destination in mind, just running – is neutral, an absolutely natural state, requiring no more effort than breathing, and a lot less effort than thinking. Unless you're some top ultramarathon runner, heading across a continent and back, that feeling can't last, but while it's there I definitely feel like I'm on to something.

Ahead of me, slightly downhill, about a mile away, was a telecommunications mast, so I made that my goal. I was concerned about having to climb back up the hill from there, but the invitation of this landmark, and the sea beyond it, was too good to resist. The village tapered away as I ran past several lovely villas, then some half-built ones, and out into open ground – beautiful, but dusty and scrubby, like the California countryside you see in old Westerns.

Running had reinvigorated my music-listening habits,

as I sought songs to fill my runs; I was listening to music more than I had in years. It was a great opportunity to listen to new stuff, but also to rediscover things I'd once enjoyed and since forgotten. I bet you've never heard of Fad Gadget, for example. He was a very cool, esoteric, peripheral presence in the Gothy synth-pop movement of the early eighties, next along on the scale from Cabaret Voltaire, early Human League and, over there in the mainstream on *Top of the Pops*, Depeche Mode. Fad Gadget broke through with the scary, mysterious yet catchy single 'Ricky's Hand'. My brother was a big fan, copying big black images from Fad Gadget's album artwork in grand scale onto his bedroom wall.

I was a sucker in my early teens – in the mid-eighties – for all the twelve-inch remixes that bands put out, particularly synth bands. The likes of Frankie Goes To Hollywood never put out one seven-inch where half a dozen twelve-inches would do – and I loved it all. It gave my young ears, newly fascinated with music, so many little details to chew on.

The winter I took that first trip to Cyprus, I'd bought – from Fopp in Nottingham – a Fad Gadget best-of CD for a fiver. I'd forgotten he'd existed, for a moment – well, for a few years, I suppose – and the monochrome cover art was so evocative. For a week or two I binge-listened to the CD in the car, then I transferred my favourites – with only a little struggle with the technology – onto my iPod.

The best tunes, and the versions I remembered, were all on the second disc – extended remixes. High up on Cyprus, as the road I was on petered out and became a rutted track, I heard 'Love Parasite II'. I hadn't realised, until that moment, how deeply you can file a musical memory. Here was a song that had completely slipped my mind, but that it turned out I knew like the back of my hand. Tunes we listen to repeatedly as youngsters are written on our mental hard drives in a kind of forensic detail we can only imagine later in life, and this time that sensation was exaggerated by the obscurity of the song – not only obscured from me by time, but also just plain obscure.

I was in the run, and in the music. The dirt track I was on curved across the headland in a wide loop around the mast, back to the road, past views of deep valleys either side, the snow-capped mountains at the centre of the island and the huge, silver-gold expanse of the Mediterranean. Meanwhile, the track I was *listening* to laid its melodic cards on the table: essentially, one big fat bassline. Synthesised and sequenced bass, so high up in the song's minimal mix that a modern music producer would think there had been some terrible mistake, pounds a repeated groove as the lyrics describe the love parasite of the title. Plot spoiler: it's a baby. Just a normal, human baby, but described in such cynical, sinister terms as to be almost unrecognisable. The music doubles down on this sense of unease, just a few ethereal noises and operatic backing vocals over the unremitting, automated bass and drums, creating a sense of enormous space – scary space. Looking at the space in front of me, it got me thinking about the space behind. I could see for miles up there in the middle of nowhere – and suddenly, that spooked me. It was like the blooming *Woman in Black*. But there weren't any snakes . . . right?

This being the extended remix of 'Love Parasite', it got even more minimal, stripping away what few sounds there were and taking its time bringing them back in, one by one. I revelled in my intimate, newly rediscovered memory of it; as only the drums kept going steadily, with unsettling snatches of those sparkly noises, I knew that that giant bassline was going to suddenly come back round, just once, as if saying 'Boo!' from behind a door. I had loved the thrill of this when I was twelve . . . and here it was. Brilliant. Not really spooky, just exciting, like a roller coaster. There weren't any snakes. Probably hardly any, anyway. Yes, as the path turned back up the hill, it got within feet of where the crumbly-looking cliffs dropped hundreds of feet to the sea, and for a moment, still running fast, I could see straight down to the waves on the beach – but I was safe here on the path.

The climb back up towards the village was gentle, and before I got all the way back I found another road that swooped down across the hill to my right, making a nice loop before the final steep downhill and home. It was a fantastic run, and one I would go on to do over and over again, but I always remember listening to 'Love Parasite II' that first time I followed the track down to the cliffs. Besides, when I ran there in the summer months, in snake season, I stayed on the roads.

Fad Gadget – real name Frank Tovey – died young, aged forty-five, in 2002. He was great – a totally committed, challenging artist who also had a fantastic sense of showbiz, from the inspiration of his performance art and design, to the simple, hooky pop sensibility that underpins even his weirdest records. I particularly love the way that, when, later in his career, he abandoned the stage name and the synthesisers, he sounded just the same. Seek him out.

Another tune like this: The other Fad Gadget track that I revel in on my playlist is 'Collapsing New People (Berlin Mix)'. There's really chunky production in this collaboration with the German group Einstürzende Neubauten, and another excellently cynical lyric, this time conflating fashionistas with vampires; plus, of course, another massive bassline.

Another run like this: The other island I've been to for work where dramatic runs up into the mountains and down to rugged cliffs over the ocean show you a whole different side to the place is Tenerife. I know – lucky me.

7. THE COAST WITH THE MOST
Southerndown 2012

There is no better beach in Britain than that at Southern-down in south Wales, looking out across Dunraven Bay and the Bristol Channel to the steep north coast of Devon and the heights of Exmoor, twenty miles away. Southern-down beach has everything: cupped in a sweep of dramatic cliffs that break up into satisfyingly chunky rocks dotted with endlessly fascinating pools full of life, then broad, flat sands and eminently surfable waves. There's even a little shop for all your ice cream and bucket-and-spade needs. To get the best from it you need clement weather and a low tide, but even this Brigadoonish quality enhances its magic. It's perfect.

Of course, you doubtless have your own opinion on this issue, bound up with your own holiday memories. The Deerings started staying in a place up the hill from the beach, in Southerndown village, in the summer of 2008 – a seismic year for us for all kinds of reasons – when the children were toddlers, and this wonderful, escapist scene very quickly wove itself into our young family's story – not just the beach, but the secret garden just inland from it, the Billie Holiday CD in the cottage, gin and tonics looking out of the window, the sun setting over the cricket pitch, and on and on.

My love of running developed in parallel with our relationship with Southerndown. The first time we went there, I didn't run at all. The next time I did, but I had no idea how far a run I'd worked out on the local OS map would turn out to be – I'd scope out what looked like a gorgeous countryside loop, set off . . . and be back in ten minutes. Over the next couple of years, in the occasional week we spent down there, my understanding of the map spread further – and the whole family's love for, and knowledge of, the area did too, with the result that the entire place contracted wonderfully. I could run up to the top of the hill, down the valley beyond, reach the pub by the ruined castle and the stepping stones that we knew and loved, then follow the river to the sea, then the rocky coastline back to our beach . . . All this countryside and seaside gorgeousness in a run no further than my regular trot down to the bank at home.

Of all the runs in this book, I think this loop – Southerndown, Heol-y-Mynydd, Ogmore, Ogmore-by-Sea,

Southerndown – might be my favourite of all. And they're all pretty special, so that's really saying something.

The only downside of running on these great holidays was that taking myself off for an hour right in the middle of the day – or the morning, at least – felt selfish, like I was missing out on quality family time. I'd still get the run in, but it was always a bit snatched – the whole point of this time away was for the four of us to spend time together. And that's before you even get to the days when we had to prep and pack a picnic, along with a bag bulging with every possible thing we might need at the beach, in time to toddle down the hill for the best of those capricious tides.

Then, in 2012, the unthinkable: the weather wasn't that great, for several days. The children, getting older would you believe, were finding their own things to do, and sometimes needed time alone to do them. I was rattling around, 'entertaining' everyone with my thoughts, plans, songs, jokes, voices and general noise . . . So, when I took myself off out into the wind and rain – well, they were all too polite to say they were relieved, but let's just say they didn't necessarily mind.

What's more, where once I had been a bit daunted by this place, I had now found my running relationship with it. This was very friendly trail running – no huge bleak expanses, no mountains to climb, just an undulating little corner of Glamorgan, with something new and gorgeous every quarter of a mile. The most challenging part was brilliantly timed; once the hill, the valley and the river were done, the rocky coastline home was an invitation. A flat, sheep-nibbled path cruises the top edge of the beach at Ogmore-by-Sea as the sand turns to chunky rocks, and those rocks gradually become small cliffs, the climb to the higher country of Southerndown beginning almost imperceptibly – before you know it, you're on a path along the top of full-sized cliffs high above the sea.

This particular blustery day, I reached the beginning of the coastal path feeling hugely energised, rattling along like a dog let off the leash. Instead of following the gradual climb, I stayed low, though I knew that sooner or later I'd have to turn more sharply up the hill, which was rising higher and higher on my left. Before long I reached a steep sward that I recognised, a gully that dropped straight down from the end of the village to the sea below, and the end of the lower path I was on – the last mile of the coast back to Dunraven Bay being a tall wall of DANGEROUS CLIFFS, as the signs along the footpath continuing along the top warned in big, red letters.

So this green, grassy tongue was my route up, and I was ready. I had some Leftfield playing, for goodness' sake; if listening to Leftfield doesn't enhance your run, check your pulse, because you could well be dead. Not only that, but this was 'Inspection (Check One)', a mid-speed chug perfect for a climb, rather than a sprint – and especially perfect for me. I am an engine-room runner; my strength is all up in my torso. I'm not one of these long-limbed, light and limber types whose loose legs will take them anywhere – it's all about my good lungs and my low heart rate. These legs are just a means to an end. As long as I slow down for it, I can work these chunky pistons and run uphill all day – a tractor, not a sports car. This Leftfield tune is the sound of that motion: viscerally squelchy electronic bass notes building very gradually over a relentless, almost 'We Will Rock You' rhythm – but with decidedly un-Queen dub beats and dismissively authoritative toasting on top. It's huge. I climbed that green ladder that I'd been setting up as a challenge with ease, and it was all down to Leftfield. Honestly, I was disappointed when I reached the top before the track had stopped – I would happily have run, slowly and chuggily, straight on up into the sky.

On a high from this musical, physical moment, and now on the high path over the cliffs, I saw our beloved bay in front of me. I followed the track as it leaves the fields and squeezes in between the beach road and the precipice – getting narrower and narrower – and it was all I could do to take it a little bit slower and beware the DANGEROUS CLIFFS, because I was flying. For the first time in days, the weather was clearing – and the tide was going out . . .

I turned left again, back up the hill and home. We would make sausage sandwiches and wrap them in foil, grab the bodyboards and pack the kids into their wet-suits, then get out there for one more beautiful day on the beach, after all.

Another tune like this: Electronic music is great for run-ning, but it's important to include mid-speed tunes like 'Inspection (Check One)' as well as the speedy bangers. 'Music:Response', by the Chemical Broth-ers, with its sequenced bleep that starts in a different place every time it plays, is another prime example.

Another run like this: I once ran from Caswell Bay beach, west of Swansea, all the way back to the city, which was a great, gentle yet beautiful coastal run, through the bays and over the hills to the Mumbles, then all the way round Swansea's enormous bay. One for the books. Not this book, though.

8. DOCK TALES

Cardiff 2013

Running in Cardiff is wonderful. Down at Cardiff Bay you can run across the Barrage to the old Custom House and beyond, up the hill to Penarth, or you can make your way past the Marina and pick up the flyover – nicer than it sounds – to complete a circuit back to Mermaid Quay; or, on the north side of the city, you can follow the River Taff through Bute Park and Pontcanna Fields – this is where Cardiff parkrun is, and it's a gorgeous one. The trail by the river carries on after that for miles, up into the Welsh countryside – and Wales is no slouch in the countryside department.

Comedians playing the Glee Club – a great comedy venue down at Mermaid Quay – used to stay in a hotel right next to an oblong body of water that was once a dock serving the Atlantic. Amazing to think of the massive ships that would once have steamed in and out of there; a big rusty crane still stands as a reminder, directly across from the hotel's breakfast room. But now it's just a big box of quiet water, perfect for running around. And birds! I've seen all sorts down there: cormorants, great crested grebe, tufted ducks, swans and more. When I first started running, this seemed the perfect spot to me – a flat rectangle, yet picturesque. The kind of place runners train in films – like something out of *Chariots of Fire* – but I don't think running in real life is quite like that. I never saw that many other runners down there, although I shouldn't think I'm the only one charmed by it; I bet someone's got it as a Strava segment.

I spent a weekend there with fellow stand-ups Barry Castagnola and Paul Tonkinson – I didn't know Paul well at the time, but our adventures together in running began that Saturday. Paul and Barry had both run the London Marathon; I had only just started running a couple of miles here and there. Even just chatting about it with them, I felt completely out of my depth – like the time I played a charity gig with, and for, vegans; I was on a vegan diet – still am – but when I played the gig I'd only been on it for a few days. In both circumstances, I felt like these true believers would smell the cheese on me.

So, when Paul and Barry said, 'Let's all run around the dock in the morning, then,' how was I going to get out of it?

'I'll be too slow for you guys.'

'We'll go whatever speed you like.'

'Then I'm all out of excuses.'

I would have to run without headphones – this terrified me. I know now that chatting and running is an equally brilliant, completely different way to distract myself from the breathing, stomping machine that is my body, but this was all new to me back then.

Aside from them being nice, inclusive guys, there was further distraction from my self-conscious, never-before-observed efforts: Barry and Paul are so interestingly different to each other as runners. Barry is shorter and stocky, Paul is long, loose and limber, and this physicality echoes their attitudes. Barry held a little bottle of water designed to be carried on a run, and judiciously set off his watch's stopwatch as we began, checking our pace along the way. Paul, in an old t-shirt and shorts almost as inappropriate for running as mine, brought nothing and worried not. This dichotomy was fascinating for me. I could see how easily I could, as a runner, grow up to be Barry, copying and even overtaking his attention to stats to the point of obsession – yet how, even though I would never be as natural a runner as Paul, his monk-like asceticism was also something to aspire to. I was basically running with the living embodiments of conscious and subconscious, left brain and right, ego and id, yin and yang . . .

But that is not this story – for two reasons. For one thing, I wasn't listening to music. Check the front of the book out – that is Off Message. For another, I did not make the distance. A loop of that old dock is somewhere between a mile and a mile and a half. I made it round once with these guys and felt good about it. Going into the second time round, I began to see that the pace was a little ambitious for me – I'd been trying to show myself at my best, of course – and that, despite all their protestations of friendly trotting, as slow as the slowest friend in the gang, they both secretly fancied a race.

So I peeled off ahead of lap three, feeling fairly energised and inspired, and made my way back to my hotel room in time to see the boys heading down the far side of the water, under the crane, Tonkinson pulling away and building a brutal lead on Castagnola. Barry's a great runner, but Paul's amazing – and *much* more competitive than he looks. I've been in races with him – but I've never raced him, and I never will. Not just because he'd win – he definitely would – but also because our friendship might not withstand the battle.

After that introduction, I ran around that water every time I stayed in Cardiff. As I became more experienced and my runs got longer, I would run out to the Bay and back, but still loop the dock at the beginning or the end. One New Year's Day, after a gig at the Glee Club followed by a full-on after-party in the dressing room with the late, legendary Ian Cognito and a champagne-fuelled after-the-after-party party with my wife back at the hotel, I crawled out early into bright sunshine and, with thick snow on the ground, made it my first run of the year. What year, I don't know, but for a morning-after-the-night-before run, it wasn't bad at all; I got it in before the hangover, I suppose. Considerably rougher was the drive back to London with an extended, unexpected detour to drop off Ian Cognito at his canal-boat home in Bristol.

Then, in 2013, I was in Cardiff for my first run – a 'recovery run', as they're known – following my second London Marathon. That's right: two marathons! I'd come a long way since that scary weekend with the real runners five years before. By this time, running was a huge part of my life. Running for charity had given shape and fervour to my hobby, and brought it crashing into my comedy gigs, where no one wants to talk running, but people are drunk and generous, and happy to be accosted by a man with a bucket who's given them a good laugh. My children, now six and eight, didn't remember me as anything other than a runner.

At that time, I would often watch films with the kids and find that they were just fantastic – the films, not the kids – although they're the best children in the world, of course. I think my children were young in a golden era of animated family films, where Pixar had set a high bar that other studios strove for and often matched – I could list you some real classics here, but I won't toy with you. Even second-string sequels were beautiful, funny, inventive entertainment we could all enjoy over and over again.

What I'm saying is I love *Madagascar 3: Europe's Most Wanted*.

At the time, I couldn't watch the sequence where the animals pull it together and create a psychedelic, Cirque du Soleil-style smash-hit circus to the uplifting strains of Katy Perry's 'Firework' without letting out a little tear. She is, of course, the go-to pop star for 'You go, girl!' empowerment, and no matter how good at that she is, familiarity breeds contempt – but this was her first crack at that, or the first I was aware of, at least, and I *loved* it. That song was going on my Best Marathon Playlist in the World . . . Ever. I would be not so much running through south-east London as shooting across the sky.

I realised a couple of things cruising round the placid, man-made lake behind Cardiff Holiday Inn Express that first weekend of May 2013. One is that, when you train for a marathon, you get fit – and stay fit. I thought I'd be a decrepit, shuffling wreck out there a week after the main event, but the truth of it was, underneath a superficial achiness, a couple of chafes and an overall feeling that I'd been through the mill, I felt good. I was cruising. I felt light, loose and, yes, very nearly limber. As I rounded the north-west corner of the rectangle, Katy Perry came on and I realised something else: my daydream had not come to pass. Among all the carefully chosen supercuts on my extensive London Marathon playlist, 'Firework' had not made an appearance. Gutted! That would have been perfect – such an empowering song, with all that colourful, positive imagery from the film that my family and I had enjoyed so much. As the song built up to its soaring chorus, I pictured them all – wife, son and daughter – just before the seventeen-mile mark, about as far from the beginning and end of the London Marathon as it is possible to be, loving me and supporting me – and all the runners – with their little home-made signs and their sweets to hand out . . . and out there, alone in Cardiff, where the big boats used to load up before puffing across the map to America, I cried and cried. I didn't just let a little tear out – I properly went.

So, maybe another symptom of recently running a marathon was a certain emotional vulnerability. Maybe you can't completely plan the songs and tunes that are going to inspire you, or when you're going to hear them. And maybe it was for the best that Katy Perry *hadn't* made an appearance on the big day, when there had been quite a few more people around.

Another tune like this: Almost anything from Taylor Swift's *1989* album – 'Shake It Off', 'Blank Space', 'Style' . . . so many great, run-friendly pop classics.

Another run like this: Along the Mersey and around the Royal Albert Dock and the Echo Arena in Liverpool: airy, iconic . . . and flat.

9. NORWEGIAN FLOOD

Oslo 2014

During the Edinburgh Fringe 2014 I had something of a comedian's career moment, the like of which you might imagine us often having but that we, in fact, seldom do. After my gig, while I was still in the post-show glow, my agent said, 'Would you like to do this?' and presented, fully formed, an international tour for not long after the festival, well paid and with a bunch of great acts.

For a moment there, I was quite literally living the dream.

It was a brief tour of Scandinavia – Trondheim, Oslo, Reykjavík, Stockholm – and it really was as great as it sounds. I'd never been to Reykjavík, which is a brilliant city and where the show was a very big, rock-and-roll affair. I had worked in Stockholm years before, in my old job – presenting English language workshops in schools for a bit of blue. The third corner of my comedian–runner triangle is that I do love a map. In the UK I'd found great runs, and enjoyed new insight into places I'd been to loads of times, by seeking out canal towpaths and river-side routes, not to mention disused railways. You imagine the ideal of running to be a wide, open space – Forrest Gump in Monument Valley comes to mind – but I know now that I prefer a city run. I root out sneaky green spaces and waterside spots – the more post-industrial the better, because then I feel like Nature and I are in on a secret; plus, they suit my attention span – there are new things to see round every corner. If I was following Forrest Gump through Monument Valley, I'd be all 'Yes, lovely stuff, but how long do I have to look at it for?'

But I had never sought out the blue line in Scandinavia before. At this point, I didn't even know this was a river – from the map, it might've been a canal, and immedi-ately I had memories of the great, flat, steady routes I'd found in Manchester, Birmingham, Edinburgh. No. To get a feel for what this run was like, you'd have to blend that idea with a healthy dose of *The Lord of the Rings*.

The water that I found fitted the bill for a run; there was a leafy path alongside it, and the river itself was interestingly engineered into a landscape of bridges, weirs and old buildings, maybe mills once upon a time – right up my post-industrial alley. But – wow. A raging torrent was coming down towards me, the like of which I'd never seen anywhere in Britain, let alone round the corner from coffee shops, internet start-ups, day care centres and all the other gear you find in a cool, redeveloped quarter of a modern city. It was a thundering wall of white water a hundred feet across; a tamed monster; the ice melt of the mountains making its awesome way to the ocean.

So, great: I was going to be running uphill. Remember, it was pouring with rain.

At this moment, my life was made almost entirely of water. But if you have to be out in the rain, running is the best way to be. From a technical point of view, your thermostat will be right up – it's going to be significantly longer before you feel in any way cold, and you and your sporty clothes will soon be dry when you're done. Plus, psychologically, it feels like a victory – you did it: you came out for a run against the odds. This persistent precipitation is just a wonderful reminder of your commitment.

Oslo was everything about committing to a run while I was away in another city for work, turned up to eleven. Not just while we were there – in the snatched hour or two I had there. Not just by the canal – next to a veritable Niagara. Not just warming myself against the rain, but climbing up an unending hill in *torrential* rain. It was fantastic.

As I climbed, the run continued to be great. My path zigzagged up through green spaces but never strayed far from the river, crossing it now and again on spindly modern footbridges, as the water below kept up its incredible blast. I probably would have enjoyed myself even without headphones, but it felt like the music I was listening to was a force field against the potential misery of the weather. Eventually, the romantically engineered path finished and I found myself running up the high street of some suburb, so I turned back – I'd gone far enough by then for that to be my halfway point.

So there I was – fully endorphined-up, running down-hill towards a shower, some dry clothes and an exciting comedy gig. When you run downhill for some distance after you've been running uphill for a while, as long as the downward slope isn't *too* steep, it doesn't feel like a hill at all – you just feel like you're the fastest, strongest runner in the world. With this mindset – flying, inside and out – I ran back onto the riverside path, and Josh Wink's 'Higher State of Consciousness' started playing. This is simple, purposeful techno. If you didn't listen to it – ideally, dance to it – in the mid-nineties, when it first came out, you would be well within your rights to respond with something along the lines of 'What the hell is this noise?' But I was there, and I did dance to it. The crazily-processed sample that gives the tune its name is a sound I've been imitating with nothing more than my lips for a quarter of a century. Yes, you've got to be in the mood for the atonal, relentless, squelchy bleep that, in time, takes over the whole track – a Roland 303 bass sequencer with the knob being manually twiddled, jazz fans – but I *was* in the mood! *Pe-pew-pew, pe-pe-pew-pew pe-pew . . . Raaargh!* There are Norwegians who still talk, even now, of the wild-eyed, big, wet, grinning Englishman who flew past them slightly above the ground that rainy afternoon all those years ago, spreading love and rainwater. The tune's build up to, and down from, euphoric, rhythmic madness was the perfect centrepiece to the euphoric, rhythmic madness of my whole run.

I shouldn't think I'm the only person my age who has repurposed the dancing music of their twenties as the running music of their forties, but I still haven't discovered as many other runners on this path as I would imagine there are out there. It's very lucky timing for a lifelong music fan and middle-aged runner – little did I know that the joyous, pulsating, love-engendering tunes I was enjoying then would, in this different context, work exactly the same way so many years later. What would once have been a rave is now a parkrun, and, in essence, the experiences are exactly the same. And so am I.

Another tune like this: 'Access' by DJ Misjah and DJ Tim – if anything, this is even more minimal than 'Higher State of Consciousness', without that stretched-out vocal sample, but what 'Access' has got is a relentless, on-the-beat squelch and the longest, most satisfying drop-down-then-build-back-up of any dance record, anywhere.

10. FAST THROUGH THE FOG

York 2014

In the early days of my running, I must have believed I had all the time in the world. I regularly allowed myself six, twelve, eighteen months' recovery between big or even medium-sized events. I made it my ambition to run the New York City Marathon 'when I'm fifty'. This was before I was forty.

Imagine the mindset I had: the lovely, wide-open idea of what I'd get round to, and when I'd get round to it. Now, given the opportunity to run a once-in-a-lifetime event, I'd say, 'Yes! Now! Quick! Before my legs give up for good!' Not just when it comes to running; in life, these days, I positively revel in the idea that time is short, that if I want to do something I should make a start now, and that, with most things, chances are I'm already too late.

To be fair, back in those days I probably considered my work far more important than my running, and only intended to devote a fraction of my time to this 'hobby'. Of course, as with any addiction, this sensibly prioritised time management soon went out of the window, but when I look back now at my running schedule from, say, 2010 to 2015, I can't imagine what I was doing with my non-running time.

I'd run two marathons, in pretty good times and without thinking about it too hard, when, blithe, innocent, speedy and still young-ish, I got round my second Royal Parks Half Marathon in less than ninety minutes. A friend of mine – an actor I'd met through work who had a sideline in training runners, i.e. someone who actually knew about this stuff – said that, if I could run a half marathon at that speed, I should be able to run a full marathon in three hours and fifteen minutes. *Wow*, I thought, *I need to get on to that*. I wasted no time, booking myself in to run one in York a snappy twelve months later.

Looking back, that was the exact moment when my running innocence began to drain away. After that half marathon, I went from not knowing that I'd run particularly fast, to being pleased with my time without much frame of reference, to feeling I ought to be training for a fast marathon – all in the space of about an hour.

Not that this meant I spent the intervening twelve

months learning the real ropes of distance running. By the time I got to York in October 2014 to take part in the Yorkshire Marathon, I was taking the task at hand pretty seriously, but I still knew very little, devising my whole training plan and, indeed, running philosophy, all on my own, without consulting anyone with any experience or doing any reading on the subject. I just ran plenty, and tried to always be going at the pace I'd need to be travelling to get twenty-six-point-two miles run in 195 minutes – less than seven and a half minutes per mile, basically. I'd newly taken to carrying my phone with me on my runs, using it to measure how far, and fast, I'd gone – a loss of innocence in itself. I only ever looked at this information once I was home, though, the phone stashed away while I was out there.

I made the huge sacrifice of taking the night off work before the marathon – a *Saturday* night; a comedian's bread-and-butter – to head up to York, where I'd set myself up in a pretty pukka hotel by booking it cheap and well in advance. I got to bed at around half nine; I didn't sleep like a baby – I had a disturbed night forcing myself to stay in bed, asleep – but I was nevertheless well rested when I woke up a little after seven the next day.

I was travelling very light – ready to run, just a couple of bits in a bag; I'd be getting the train home pretty much straight after the marathon. As I strolled through York city centre to the station to catch the shuttle bus that would take me up to the start of the race, I realised that I was somewhat underdressed for a Yorkshire morning in October. It was only just getting light, through a damp, Dickensian fog, and by the time I took my seat on the bus I was shivering uncontrollably.

On the university campus, where the event is based, I found a spot where I could cosy up a bit and comforted myself with the thought that when the sun got right up in the sky it would warm off the fog. I prepared myself for the race ahead. This was my third marathon, so I did know *some* things; I had a proper pair of runners' Lycra shorts by now – not a shonky, tweedy-looking four-pound pair from a market stall in Thailand – three or four carbohydrate gels in my pocket to boost my energy when whatever natural food-fuel I had in me ebbed away over the miles, and plasters on my nipples. That's one very important thing I'd learned the hard way.

At the start line, the sun was not in evidence, the fog very much still present. As we waited to get going, my body temperature quickly dropped to the level it had been on the shuttle bus, i.e. mildly hypothermic. *Let's go, already!* Phew – we were off.

It was cold, the start is downhill, and I was in among a bunch of very keen runners and a couple of international athletes. We went off like a pack of greyhounds. We dropped down through central York, where the towers of the Minster were disappearing into low cloud, and the near-monochrome mistiness really appealed to the Goth in me. My music player immediately responded by playing 'A Forest' by the Cure – that famous, cyclical riff and bassline rolling like my busy legs as Robert Smith's dreamy, paranoid guitar and lyrics floated over them. *Superb accidental virtual DJing*, I thought, doffing an imaginary cap to my teeny-tiny music player as I fell in with a pack of steady runners who felt like they were of a pace with me and we made our way out of town.

Now, irritatingly early – around two miles in – I needed a wee. This turns out to be a habit of mine, and I've made my peace with it now – but I didn't know that yet, and it panicked me. I dived into a little plastic cubicle; I didn't literally dive, of course – have you been in these things at festivals? – but I was in and out of there in twenty, twenty-five seconds. Nevertheless, predictably enough, a huge bunch of runners passed me as I hopped across the pavement, back onto the course. *Gah!* I thought, as I spotted a flag flapping in the pack – it was a pacer, one of the flag-carrying runners you can follow to set yourself at the right speed to achieve whatever time you're going for, from a like-the-wind two and a half hours right through to a quite-hard-enough-thank-you-very-much four and a half. *Those people are with the 3:15 guy!* They were hardly ahead of me, but in the fog they were already nearly out of sight. I didn't catch them, but I stayed with them.

My music player, meanwhile, was taking the mickey a bit. I had some very stark, early-eighties synth in Cabaret Voltaire's 'Yashar', then more Cure, with 'Disintegration', a great howl of a song, excellent for running, Robert Smith very much re-establishing his misery credentials after the pop years, and 'Wide Open Space' by Mansun, which was from the nineties rather than the eighties, but didn't buck the stylistic trend.

Yes, admittedly, I had put all these songs on the playlist – I had been that teenager, and this was my midlife . . . moment – but they were by no means all that was on there; it was a collection that encompassed joyous music, loads of house, film soundtracks, bombastic rock and pop, hip hop, drum and bass, all sorts. That morning in Yorkshire it magically caught the mood, playing whatever the teen me within needed to hear to keep pounding those spooky lanes, as we left the city behind and clusters of homes at the roadside became fewer and farther between. I felt like Jodie Foster as Clarice Starling, sprinting through the woods at the beginning of *The Silence of the Lambs*. We haven't met the baddies yet but, already, an unnamed dread is on her tail.

It was a fun psychological chill to match the fairly motivating actual chill out there in the country. As we spread out a bit and pressed on, out of the villages, through the fields and into some forest, the fog thickened, and as we ran towards the ten-mile mark, I could only really see one person ahead of me, a guy in broad red-and-white horizontal stripes, top and shorts. He looked a little like a Victorian swimmer, and though, doubtless, his kit was some completely respectable club or sports gear, my panicky competitiveness tagged him as someone who couldn't possibly be running faster than me – making it strange that I couldn't catch him up.

It seemed to take for ever to pass this guy as just the two of us cruised through that foggy forest; it was like the rest of the marathon – the rest of the world – was just a vague memory. There was just me, stripy boy, and the big grey beyond. I had begun to think that my pertinent playlist of edgy, spiky doom had run its course, but this was the moment when it peaked – 'Bela Lugosi's Dead' by Bauhaus played. What drama! To paraphrase Spinal Tap, you have to ask yourself how much more Goth Pete Murphy's ghoulish, post-Bowie-voiced eulogy to the star of the film *Dracula* could be, and the answer would be: none more Goth.

I don't think people's first thoughts, if I were to say 'running music', would be this kind of thing, but 'Bela Lugosi's Dead' is absolutely great to run to. The spacious-ness of the minimal production, the generous, psychedelic time created by the extended mix and the steady, repeti-tive, kick-drum beat, all underpinning vocals and guitar that gradually build to the drama levels of a mini opera – it's a blend that will get you there, albeit in a chilly, black-and-white way. And I was already somewhere cold and sinister. The combined effect was perfect.

The trees cleared, and gradually the fog, too. The Yorkshire Marathon halfway point, well marked with a big clock, is right out in the countryside, and that first time it felt like a staging post on the other side of the galaxy. After that, the mood of the route changes as you pick up the A64. The countryside is still beautiful, but everyone's running straight now, with clear purpose – woodland wandering is over. This was particularly clear that first time, as my black-fingernailed, backcombed, spooky daydream came to an end.

I had given up on catching the pacer-centric pack that had passed me at the Portaloo, but I wasn't far behind them, and as we went round the switchback at the furthest point of the course, on the outskirts of Stamford Bridge, I saw them coming back towards me.

But it wasn't the 3.15 pacer I could see at the heart of the group – it was the 2.59 pacer.

I told you I didn't know what I was doing.

Well, I'd heard that going off too fast was a risk, and here was some pretty solid evidence that I'd done it. What's more, I seemed to be slowing down, as people I'd passed in the first half – including stripy boy – were now trickling back past me. *Ah well,* I thought, *I'm going as fast as I can, it feels like I'm making the same pace as before, and what's done is done.* I hung in there. Note how helpful all my naivety-based mistakes were! This was another: checking my phone later, I saw that my pace at this point was – sure enough – completely steady. The people I clocked passing me after the halfway point were trying for a 'negative split' – speeding up a little in the ambitious, focused hope that they could run the second half of the marathon faster than the first.

Good luck with that . . . I had no idea. I just plodded on.

I had a carbohydrate gel at around fifteen miles; *groo*, it didn't half make me feel queasy, but after that I could feel the energy boost, so I got another one down at around twenty-one miles. I was beginning to run just slightly slower, but not much – I didn't really have a slower gear in those days; it was just 'keep going' or 'stop' – and I was Not . . . Going . . . To . . . Stop. I remember going for the third gel at around twenty-four, twenty-five miles, and really fumbling with my little zipped-up back pocket to get it – the zip stuck – but I absolutely would not, did not, break stride. Me wrestling that little sachet out of a tiny aperture in those tight, tight shorts as I plugged on must have been quite the sight. I shouldn't have bothered – I was nearly there anyway – but maybe the blast of body basics it gave me was just the thing to get me up the dastardly hill the Yorkshire Marathon folk have in the last half-mile before the finish.

And then I was done. The moment I crossed the line I

really regretted that final gel; my crampy, queasy guts were in a right state. But from here I think I can let the gels off the hook a bit; when you go out and run the best part of thirty miles as fast as you can, it has an interesting effect on your body as it reconfigures itself to conserve and produce energy for this huge new task you're asking of it. In my experience, even without sports energy supplements, the digestive system kind of mothballs itself, and the moment you stop running it feels very odd – crampy and queasy, but in a way that doesn't seem to have much to do with food.

But what did all that matter? I'd done it. Three hours, fourteen minutes and seven seconds. At the time, I didn't really respect the moment, immediately hatching plans to run one better, faster . . . but that's OK; we can't expect to see ourselves peaking. And I really was peaking; that was, and will very likely always be, my fastest marathon.

And all because I, Jodie Foster, got chased through the foggy woods by a bunch of Goths.

Another tune like this: A slice of doom that sounds surprisingly energising when you're out on the trail is 'Dead Souls' by Joy Division: almost triumphant, if it wasn't so miserable.

Another run like this: All the grey, northern running in the film *The Loneliness of the Long Distance Runner*.

11. COMETH THE HOUR, COMETH THE BAND

Bath 2015 and the Morvern Peninsula 2018

My listening tastes, in life and running, are very diverse, as may have already become clear.

But if I had to listen to one band on all my runs from this day forward, it would probably be Public Service Broadcasting. In fact, I like them even more as a band to enjoy when not running – live, on vinyl, all that stuff. But in terms of what I need when I'm out on the trail – or bimbling through a city centre – they do offer quite the package. Like all the dance music I have on my playlist, they offer rhythms, riffs and layered grooves that are easy to motor along to – but like all the deeply uncool prog rock I also have on my playlist, they offer ornate guitar work, interesting time signatures and a general sense of excellent musicianship at play. Their greatest trick – for any listener, sedentary or mobile – is to take their patchwork of historical samples of people talking, and give it the full sense of dynamics and drama which people generally get from sung lyrics. If I hear one of their tracks while I'm running I can treat it as a song, or give myself up to the documentary narrative; I get the option either to mentally sing along, as it were, or to visualise that content, as if I'm running while listening to a movie.

I don't know about you, but when I listen – really listen – to music on headphones, I'm basically reframing my actual life as a film, with whatever's playing as the soundtrack. I'm not alone in this, am I? Even more so when I'm running, because I'm forgetting about the day-to-day, logistical realities of life, tiring out and dialling back the rational side of my mind, and loosening up into a distracted, slightly dreamy mental state. Plus, I bloody love a film. It wasn't watching Mo Farah run that set me on this road, or Paula Radcliffe or Elihud Kipchoge – it was Forrest Gump, Ethan Hunt from *Mission: Impossible* and 'Babe' Levy, the marathon man from *Marathon Man*, that inspired me to run. And Jason Bourne. Jason Bourne most of all – motoring along the beach in Goa at the beginning of *The Bourne Supremacy*. That's the runner I aspire to be – and the runner I sometimes have to remind myself Matt Damon was only pretending to be.

So, like the film themes I have on my playlist, I come to Public Service Broadcasting for that powerful sense of the filmic – visual, dramatic storytelling slightly beyond the normal sense of what a 'song' is. A filmic moment on a run listening to music is a delicate thing. Like a rainbow-swirly soap bubble, just as you're marvelling at its beauty, it can pop and disappear in an instant. Once, I was running through quintessential English countryside in golden, late-afternoon sunshine; it was August, in Somerset. Gorgeousness. My phone was playing me the main theme from *Inception*, building as it does from four simple notes to enormous, revelatory, drawn-out blasts of brass – the sound of starey-eyed Leonardo DiCaprio seeing every level of his own subconscious and coming out on the other side . . .

Wait a minute, I thought, *I've lost the path.*

Suddenly, I wasn't striding purposefully, orchestrally through a hyper-real iteration of my own perception of some pastoral idyll – I was just standing, alone and slightly confused, in a field dotted liberally with cowpats.

Pop!

Listening to Public Service Broadcasting leads to an increased rate of movie-like moments while running, heightening my chance of really enjoying those moments without necessarily remembering who and where I am, and feeling like a fool.

The first time I did the Bath Half Marathon, for example, one of their songs played a very dramatic role. The event is an absolutely perfect warm-up for the London

Marathon – one month before, big and volubly supported, full of charity runners of all ages and abilities, weaving in and out of the iconic architecture of the city. But – and perhaps I'm stating the obvious here – half the distance.

The course travels to and from a five-mile loop that you go around twice. That first time I did the course, I set off at some speed, but I was sort of in control of it, and I held on. As I pulled into the second of those laps – so, around halfway through the Half – I had a bit of a moment. The course climbed up from the river and through the heart of the city, hooking around picturesque Queen Square and heading west. As I came up the slope into the square, and rounded the corner where the Parkinson's UK supporters were cheering in front of Jane Austen's old house, I experienced a fuzzy sort of high listening to the Public Service Broadcasting song 'The Other Side', a high which combined the joy of speeding along and being cheered, with the slightly desperate physical feeling of going up a not-insignificant hill, seven miles into a fast run. The song kept this feeling positive, turning my potential vulnerability into grinning happiness and giving me the opportunity to identify with real-life NASA astronaut Jim Lovell, who, in this track from the band's album *The Race for Space*, embarks on a dangerous slingshot mission around the moon. So, y'know, a lot like me running around Bath.

I was going well enough that I really didn't want to stop and lose valuable seconds, but coming out of the square I had to admit to myself that I needed to go to the toilet – so, I'd have to break this pace, and this magical musical moment, by nipping into the cubicle coming up on my left. I know – another cubicle story; just be thankful that I'm not one of those runners who, er, *does without* cubicles. And I'll keep it brief – just as I did in Bath in fact. As I broke stride and stepped into the plastic box, Jim Lovell's craft went round behind the dark side of the moon and Mission Control lost radio signal – as planned, but nevertheless a time of great danger and trepidation, as Earth waited for the astronaut to re-establish contact. The band build this tension brilliantly, and no matter how many times you hear the cathartic burst of music as Jim comes back on line, you never stop wanting to punch the air with joy and relief.

My own cathartic burst coincided perfectly with NASA's loss of signal, and on my return to the race I did indeed nearly punch the air with joy and relief. The synchronicity didn't so much burst my bubble as draw a clown face on it, as my musical, movie-like high continued – but became ridiculous, with Jim Lovell's adventure aggrandising my wee and my blue plastic Davlav becoming one with his lonely capsule in the dark vacuum of space.

Was this a movie moment or did I feel a fool? Both: it was a draw.

I'll tell you, later on, the story of a quasi-religious moment I experienced on the Morvern Peninsula out on the west coast of Scotland and how part of my joy that day was familiarity with the spot – but that was when I ran there for a second time. My first run there was also special, but not quite so immaculate.

I was on another family holiday, this time in a landscape that's on a somewhat grander scale than the Deerings' favourite corner of South Wales. The day was grey, and I felt the weight of the mileage; I was fit, but not quite as fit as I wanted to be. The long, slight incline that led for two miles from the village where we were staying to a gate out onto moorland really took it out of me – and it was *early*. I'd got out first thing so as not to miss too much family-holiday time. At least I'd have the glorious Caledonian countryside to myself. As I got to the deer-proof gate out onto open land, I turned – and realised there was a pickup truck following me with a couple of builders in it. They must've been stuck staring at my plodding, Lycra-shiny little caboose for fifteen, twenty minutes. The lucky devils.

I let them go, passing them half an hour later as they built some kind of farm building in a stupendously picturesque spot. Actually, they were drinking coffee and eating what looked like bacon rolls, but I'm sure they got some work done in the end. I climbed, properly uphill now, to the point where the track I was on began to follow the northern edge of the peninsula. As it levelled off, the matt grey waters of Loch Sunart spread out below me on my left, with huge, ominous-looking mountains rising straight up from the far shore. Flat though it now was, my road was long – it zigged and zagged in and out of small valleys as streams cut through the escarpment heading for the water below. Scotland is just enormous, particularly to a London-based looper of little parks and local alleyways.

The extreme Scottishness of my situation, already palpable, went up a notch when I rounded one bend to find the road full of scary, long-haired, long-horned Angus cattle. *Toto, I don't think we're in Hackney any more.* I had a look to see whether I could climb the wall and circumnavigate them: no – that way, death by nettles would be my fate. I ran apologetically towards the fearsome beasts and luckily they were aware of the cliché: they were more afraid of me than I was of them.

They ran ahead of me for some distance. I felt terrible. What if I bumped into the farmer? *Sorry, mate, I stampeded your livestock into the sea* – but they reached a gateway they seemed familiar with and turned left onto the hillside, immediately looking terrifying again as they slowed down and gave me the eye. 'Sorry,' I said to them out loud, 'but stay in there till I come back past, all right?'

I got used to the idea that I'd be following this brilliant, epic trail for a while. A Public Service Broadcasting song came on – 'E.V.A.', also from *The Race for Space*, which counters the adventure of 'The Other Side' with the dramatic story of the first-ever space walk, as a Russian cosmonaut leaves not just the Earth, but his capsule. Once again, they deftly wield the deep drama of a breakdown as all the instruments and voices stop, except for one plangent piano slowly picking out six high chords. At exactly the moment these soaring, lonely notes played, I came round a corner and found myself at the top of the world. My track cut through a huge line of crags I had been unaware of just a moment before, running above them on the hillside. With a quick left–right I broke through the line of rock and began to descend across the front of this steep flank of the land. Hanging in space on that second corner, hundreds of feet above the water, where one white yacht bobbed in the grey, and commanding an unsurpassable view of the mountains and valleys ranged along the far side of the loch, was a bench. Sitting on it didn't catch the power of the moment, and would mean getting up again. I stood on it, bestriding the scene like a colossus.

Pling . . . Pling . . . Pling . . .

Even if I'd known this was where I was heading, arriving would still have taken my breath away. As it was, the complete surprise of this incredible, darkly beautiful, lonely place was a moment I knew I would remember with awe my whole life. And that piano!

Pling . . . Pling . . . Pling . . .

Nothing popped my bubble. This was real drama to match any film. You should have been there – but if you had been, it wouldn't have been the same. It was my solitary moment, up there all alone in space. Just me – and Public Service Broadcasting.

Another tune like this: The whole PSB canon is riven through with great running music, but *The Race for Space* is the album to start with. Check out the mighty, funky, riffy 'Gagarin' or the excitement and tension of 'Go!'.

Another run like this: A much smaller but similarly dramatic route in the Lake District takes you from Buttermere steeply up towards the high peaks of the Grasmoor group of mountains and then left along the ridge of Rannerdale Knotts to its peak at the far end, with Crummock Water spreading below you on the left and the mountains Red Pike, High Stile and High Crag ranged beyond.

12. SIDE BY SIDE ON THE BANKS OF THE CLYDE

Glasgow 2015

That last story shows, and we'll see again later, that running on the Morvern Peninsula can be a borderline religious experience for me. But it's not just that one wonderful spot; I absolutely love running in Scotland. It's got everything I look for, and a little more; my regular parkrun – Hackney Marshes – is flat and fast, with lovely people and big skies, but Aberdeen parkrun also looks out across sandy beaches to the North Sea. I have had beautiful, special country runs in the South Downs, the Lake District and South Glamorgan – but out on that west coast of Scotland the view stretches further than any I can see in England or Wales, and for me in particular, the whole place has that special magic of being really far away.

Edinburgh and Glasgow both have the three qualities I cherish in a city run: they have comedy clubs that I love to play; they both have the kind of Industrial Revolution geography that has aged into the perfect environment for runners – canal towpaths, old railway lines, municipal parks; and they have that urban magic trick where nature – greenery, water, rock – sneaks in and around the streets and buildings in surprising, secret ways. And, because it's Scotland, the drama is amped up; sure, there's a disused railway near me in north London, but the Innocent Railway in Edinburgh is one of the oldest in the world, and takes you past a mountain to the sea. At home I can follow the River Lea down to the Olympic Park, but if I follow the River Kelvin in Glasgow, it takes me down a leafy gorge, past huge, Gothic, pointy museums, university buildings and monuments, and the river itself thunders white and frothy, like the meltwater from a glacier, down to the mighty Clyde.

See? Everything I look for and a little more.

And the Clyde itself is really special. Alongside it, south-west of the city centre, the shipyards have been repurposed as a media hub, TV studios, huge gig venues and the like – shiny new buildings, and a bridge, next to far older structures that once housed machinery that was almost mythically enormous and strong. Slicing west–east on the north embankment from there, between the road and the water, the path takes you under all the bridges where traffic and trains head south, and then, past the formal gardens of Glasgow Green, out on through the leafiest edges of the eastern suburbs of Scotland's biggest city. A gorgeous, steady yet changing route for a run, and all the while the wide, black waters of the river at your elbow.

One grey but mild morning in early spring 2015, I took this route, running down to the Clyde from my hotel in the West End and turning left upstream, away from Glasgow Harbour, through the centre of town and east. I love running by water; maybe it's just practical – the air's probably good there, right? – or maybe it's primal, some deep prehistorical attraction to the source, the great flow of the world . . . Whatever, it's good for the soul. And the Clyde is so still, dark and deep; it's got – for want of a better word – charisma; running alongside it is like running with a friend. A big, scary friend who doesn't say anything. This is the balance of the place: part spiritual, part practical. The river itself is a therapeutic presence in a way that's hard to define; the path next to it is wide and flat and not too busy.

I ran a fair way that morning. I was aiming for miles rather than pace – with a third London Marathon coming up, I wanted to do at least ten – but the invitation of the path, the challenge of the water, and maybe the fact that I was just going out and back, meant that, with just a little nudge from my playlist, I went really fast.

I have a certain lack of imagination with regard to pace. Whatever speed I'm going, after the first mile or two of a run, my body will unquestioningly sustain it for the foreseeable – so a longer run where I inadvertently take it at a bit of a nip can become very handy training, an almost accidental taste of what it feels like to do that thing my co-podcaster Paul Tonkinson says is required to run a good marathon: 'Go really fast when you're tired.' Wise words.

Something mildly mind-bending takes place when you leave Glasgow this way and then reverse your route. While the Clyde abides on one side, the other is like a cross between a geography lesson and the fast–slow–fast elastic energy of a bungee jump, the bustle of the city's central business district, and the traffic on the bridges, easing a little as you go through the still-vibrant park, slowing right down to the steady quiet of the countryside the further you get down the riverside path ... Then back: sedate by the river, fun in the park, busy-busy-busy in the city. That speedy day, the effect was exacerbated by how quickly I got to each new stretch; by the time I got back to town, I was pumped. During the final straight, on the Clyde Walkway, just south of the heart of the city, a guy overtook me. Since I was going pretty fast, this got my attention. I didn't run after him – well, I did, but only because, you know, he was now in front of me and we were running in the same direction. But I tried not to speed up in a competitive way. On the other hand, I certainly didn't slow down; I wanted to be sure this fellow had made the right decision in passing me.

At around this time, Underworld's 'Born Slippy' began to play. If you're anything like the same age as me, you'll know it – the banger with the lager chant from the *Trainspotting* soundtrack, a huge mid-nineties anthem. I remember, at the end of the year the film came out, this being the tune that played at midnight on New Year's Eve – must have been 1996 into '97. I was at the Dogstar bar in Brixton; it was an incredible night. Although someone was sick on my coat.

In my head, by the river nearly twenty years later, I chuckled. What a superb running tune; so subtle, yet simple, the big, echoing chords clearing to reveal the thumping, clattering, unstoppable beats beneath. It's the sound of pure forward motion, and between it and being overtaken, there was no chance I was slowing down. And what juxtaposition! This Scottish guy – I'm assuming he was Scottish because he was running in Glasgow, even though I was and I'm not, but let's go with it – didn't have headphones in and he was sporting a club running vest. He was a great runner, rattling along, long-strided and steady, and, though I told myself he probably hadn't come as far as me, he might well have done – he certainly looked like he could go all day. He had made the right decision in passing me, of course, but he was only going a *little* faster than me, and I was pleased to see he was running hard, going for time. This was not just another of my assumptions – I saw him checking his watch. A lot. He looked at his watch about every twenty, thirty seconds. I could go mad doing that, but hey, it worked for him – one person's huge dance anthem is another person's sports watch.

Without even noticing, I missed my route off to the right, back to my hotel – and now I really was following this other runner, even as I admitted to myself that the ego boost I needed – basically, him stopping either through sheer exhaustion or from reaching the end of what I hoped was his shorter, sprintier run – was never going to happen. As we cruised over the shiny, new Clyde Arc bridge to the south-west, the song finished, I let him go – and let *it* go. Once he was out of sight, and the moment had passed, I turned back again, over the mighty, surly river.

I love how that man and I travelled alongside each other for a moment there, in Glasgow and in life. Running in the same direction, in the same place, at the same speed – all right, nearly the same speed; an Englishman and a Scotsman – all right, we don't know he was a Scotsman; one an athlete with all the right kit, making the effort to use and control his carefully trained body; the other running fast by mistake, mainly due to repetitive beats. But for a moment, the result was the same, and so were we.

'Born Slippy' is not the track that plays over the opening scene in *Trainspotting* – Renton and Spud leathering it away from the record-shop security guy, dropping their shoplifted CDs all over the pavement – that's 'Lust for Life', of course, by Iggy Pop. And they're not in Glasgow, they're in Edinburgh. And they're not running for fitness – they're on heroin for goodness' sake – but all that wrongness only added to the shonky magic of the moment for me, and played into my wider, inexplicably powerful, lifelong love for Scotland – not just as a place to run in; the whole Caledonian deal.

That night, at the brilliant Stand Comedy Club, I told the crowd how much I loved their city, and their country, and joked that when citizens of the place hear my English, middle-class accent, that love is always instantly reciprocated. And at the end of my set I performed my one-man cover version of 'Born Slippy', and had a one-man rave, live on stage. I'm not sure to what extent the audience realised how much heartfelt truth there was in my performance – a gurning, flailing, half-naked dance to the sound of one's own voice is a funny kind of love letter – but I think they appreciated it.

Another tune like this: The *Trainspotting* soundtrack was the album that made me realise that a curated set-list by a variety of artists could be as cohesive and meaningful as the work of one band or solo performer. 'For What You Dream Of' by Bedrock featuring KYO is a less famous track from it than Underworld's 'Born Slippy' but, if anything, it bangs even harder.

Another run like this: The banks of the Tyne – Newcastle or Gateshead side – make a wonderful place to run; inland from town, then back past the broad waters towards the many and varied bridges.

13. DOUBLE DROPPING THE DUST

London and Powys 2015

At this point, I'd like to tell you about 'Gold Dust' by DJ Fresh, featuring Ce'cile – a perfect running tune, not because it has anything to do with running, but because it's a blast of pure energy.

When I'm trying to run further and further, upping my mileage ahead of some event, I head south and east. From my home in London on the borders of Hackney and Islington, it's a picturesque, downhill mile to the Regent's Canal, and once I'm on the towpath I can follow it all the way down through Bethnal Green to the Thames at Limehouse Basin or fork east along the Hertford Union Canal towards the Olympic Park, where I can head north, through and around Hackney and Walthamstow Marshes, all the way – if I'm dreaming big – to Tottenham IKEA and beyond.

With just four weeks left before that third London Marathon in 2015, I was out one Sunday, looping around these green spaces and waterways, trying to rack up twenty miles. It was a sunny day, and there were plenty of people about, it being a weekend, which made it feel like less of a lonely quest, and I was, of course, listening to great music. After a couple of hours plodding along, I risked a look at my phone to see how far I'd come – I was returning west along the Hertford Union Canal; if I'd done seventeen, eighteen miles I could just head on towards home.

I'd only done fifteen miles.

Gah! Luckily – it's a skewed version of luck, but bear with me – I was just on the stretch of towpath over the fence from Victoria Park; it would be as easy as anything to pop in at the next gate, run the perimeter, then crack on home. OK, it's also a skewed version of 'easy as anything', but I could do it and I knew it, and the park was right there – like an invitation.

Victoria Park is a classic municipal space: formal gardens with pretty flowerbeds, broad swards of well-cared-for grass, long-established trees, a lake with a fountain, bandstands, the whole deal – it's really lovely. It's also full of history: there are some odd stone benches at one end that, it turns out, used to be part of the old London Bridge; in the Second World War the whole place was repurposed as a major gun battery, a key part of London's defences during the Blitz; and I filmed a cider advert in there once.

I turned into the park and then right, following the edge anti-clockwise. A road goes round on the inside, traffic-free and tree-lined, but I, being fussy about going *all the way* round, stuck even closer to the fence, following what turned out to be a really beautiful grassy track, with views down the canal on my right, and across the park to my left. It was a real treat: I absolutely love my local equivalent – Stoke Newington's Clissold Park – but I know it like the back of my hand; Victoria Park is too far away for my family and me to visit on foot, so all these undiscovered riches were just sitting there, waiting for me, that Sunday. And that was when 'Gold Dust' played. I'd refreshed my playlist for this period of training, so obviously I'd made the decision to put this song on there, but this was the first time it had dropped while I was out. What a blast! Superfast post-drum-and-bass beats, a syncopated synth-pulse melody that treads the wonderful, wild line between positive and psychotic – and that's all before the machine-gun, statement-of-intent lyric. I've said it before, and I'll say it again: *Raaargh!* What a gift it was, what a reward for the resolve I'd shown taking that turn in through the park gates – just like the pretty path I'd discovered.

I rode my new favourite tune down that track like a motorbike. And when it was done, just three poptastic minutes later, I did something I can't remember doing with any other song on any of my runs – I played it again.

The blast couldn't last forever; by the time I got to the lake, a tune or two later, I was feeling very fuzzy – deliriously, thirstily daydreaming about the cider I had once spent the day there plugging, while knowing in my heart that in real life it might not be the perfect, most isotonic beverage at that point. But in a long run, any mile a song carries you down is a gimme, a mile run without suffering that you will not have to run again.

Flash forward a couple of months to August 2015: London Marathon long completed, summer holidays under way, and me running in the Welsh hills. Real, rugged country in place of a park, sheep instead of Sunday strollers, wind and rain instead of sunshine. I was still in the post-marathon-runners' glow, where, after an event and a week or two recovering, you suddenly realise that you're still fit – all that training you did for that one day is still with you, a gift that you get to keep, like a posh costume from a show you were in that you get to take home once it's over.

We were house-sitting for friends in their heavenly home in the depths of Wales and it was fantastic – we weren't just using their house; we were living their life, and it was the high one – but my wife and I had the freelancers' problem: you can't go on holiday when you've got work. She'd been commissioned to pitch not one but several books, and I had to learn to sing and play twenty songs for a stint with the band at the Edinburgh Festival's famous *Late 'n' Live* show the following week. So while the kids played and read, and watched the skies for a chance to go out in the garden, she hunkered down over her tablet and I twanged and bellowed in a room far enough away that, well, they could all still hear me, but I wasn't quite so loud. And we both worshipped at the altar of the unmerciful god that is Welsh Hills Wi-Fi.

There's always time for a run, though, and it always helps, so there I was, out circumnavigating the valley that the house looks out across. Down through the fields, through a tiny hamlet and over a stream went the lane, before climbing, and climbing, and climbing, out of the valley and gradually away from any houses or tarmacked roads or even fields, up along the swell of a moorland ridge to the distant skyline. Any and all of the cobwebs of life were bracingly blown from me, and as I finally reached the highest point on what was now a stony, lonely track, 'Gold Dust' played once more. What a rush – but, funnily enough, it brought those work thoughts right back in, because I was going to be singing it with the band. I flew down the far side of the hill, trying in my head to keep up with the relentless flow of the lyrics and hoping that our gigs would have even a fraction of the party perfection that they represent – all hands-in-the-air, climbing-up-the-speakers, under the total control of the singer.

Yeah, I could do that.

I was running full pelt, picturing myself at – all right, master of – the club night to end all club nights, sweaty, hedonistic and pumping . . . when I stopped. At a standstill, headphones out: time to turn back. I remembered with some force that I was not in a packed-out nightclub, or an Edinburgh music venue, in the last, most bacchanalian hours before dawn. I was alone on a wind-and-rainswept moor with only some frightened sheep and busily spinning wind turbines for company. Although hedonism – and sweat – were still very much present, in their way.

I listened to the song again, again – this time for revision purposes rather than sheer running power – and let it lead me back over the bump and into the beginning of the long trot back downhill, magical scenery rolling away from me for miles in every direction, and I felt like lord of all the world.

Just as I had made it to twenty miles all those months before, I made it to Scotland with a working knowledge of those songs, and my band and I really did keep a dance floor filled with carefree, flailing dancers while the rest of the city crawled to bed and slept.

But those running moments on the way – a pretty path through an unfamiliar park, a long, satisfying, wuthering hill, a bold decision to take the long way home, a break from working hard in a rained-in house – they're like gold dust.

14. GETTING A GOOD TIME
Highbury Fields 2015

As you might remember, my very first half marathon had an incredible climax – musically. I made it through the eleven mile doldrums with the assistance of Muse – specifically the sci-fi rock histrionics of their song 'Plug In Baby' – then things heated up. As I hammered along the last, slightly uphill straight to the finish, I was borne aloft on the wings of the song 'Hang On In There Baby' by Johnny Bristol. If you don't know the track, you might be thinking, 'How apposite, Johnny encouraging Rob to hang on in there, just when he needed to hear it most,' but if you're familiar with it, you'll know that it was less . . . directly relevant.

That's because it's a sexy song. I'm not overstating this; it's not just romantic – it's saucy. So, really, my initial response when it played that day was, 'Not now, Johnny,

I'm busy.' But here's the interesting bit: it still helped. Because it's a song full of love and positivity, and driving rhythms, that builds and builds to a tremendous climax. The key change in the huge, orchestral instrumental break is transcendent; all right, orgasmic – same thing, I suppose. And the ridiculousness of this mild mismatch helped me over the line, too – with a big smile on my face. Actually 'a big smile on my face' is true most of the time I'm awake; I'm just saying it was a joyous moment.

You might think music that's appropriate for romance – or more than romance – would be inappropriate for exercise, but it's a fine line. A certain British prudishness makes talking about it excruciating – I can only apologise – but I don't think there's any shame in a bit of raunch on a running playlist. They're all different activities, but they're all physical, and I'd certainly rather run listening to a track that lacks a certain propriety but has a good beat than something featuring the sensible voice of a sports scientist over the click of a heart-rate-based metronome.

One of the earliest hits on my running music player was Missy Elliott's 'Get Ur Freak On'. Its spare, spooky production helped me along by basically making me feel a bit paranoid, and the groove is so fast that I left whatever bogeymen I'd conjured for dust. I remember running into some mist on a Welsh hill listening to it and feeling genuinely shaken – prickles-on-the-back-of-the-neck stuff.

Then one day in 2015 I heard Lauren Laverne play

Missy E's 'Can't Stop' on the radio – an enormous machine of a song. I'm a big fan of Missy Elliott, but I'd forgotten all about this particular track, which is just what you want from the radio – the familiar, when you least expect it. I slapped it on my running playlist there and then, not really listening to what Lauren was saying about how, despite a few judicious dropouts, it was still a little too spicy for daytime radio.

The next Saturday, or perhaps the Saturday after that, I went to my first ever parkrun – my closest, Highbury Fields. I love Highbury Fields; throughout my life it's a place that's represented aspiration – a glimpse of a life I want and very nearly have. When I was in my early twenties, living in the country town where I finished secondary school after my family moved out of London when I was a teenager, I splashed out on a prestigious drama course which took me to Highbury for three weeks of high-end afternoon workshops among a sample group of the up-and-coming great-and-good of UK and international performance. There were people there from all over the world and I still see some of them turn up on stage and screen from time to time.

But I couldn't afford it. Every day, the only way I could get to town was to blag a lift from my friend Luke's dad, Ken, who commuted to the distant end of the Underground, then get a travel card and cross London at my leisure. I could only afford the travel cards by not spending any money on food; my flatmates must have wondered where all their bread was disappearing to.

Ken also gave a lift to a lovely guy who wasn't allowed to drive because of a medical condition – a pitiable little carpool. I sat in the back reading, until I realised that it made me carsick; there's a nasty accident at the beginning of Chaim Potok's book *The Chosen*, and reading about that that while sailing up the serpentine sway of the M40 was a disastrous combination, the thought of which still makes me feel a bit queasy now. It was definitely pure politeness that kept me from making a mess of Ken's car that day.

I'd arrive at Highbury Fields at about half ten in the morning, then kick back there for four hours until my course started at two. It's a really beautiful place, and the weather, thank goodness, was consistently lovely – but wow, that was a whole bunch of time with myself. I got through a fair few charity-shop books, decided London was too scary and unwelcoming for me, and gradually realised that I wasn't going to get anything out of the course. It was a good course – the sense of it is something I live by to this day – but the famous, drunken old French clown running it lit on a half dozen favourites early on and the rest of us just watched him abuse – sorry, tease; sorry, teach – them every day. Meanwhile, I made some friends among the beautiful people in the class, but nothing much beyond small talk.

I think I just looked a bit too hungry.

When the love of my life led me back to London a few years later, I realised that it's only scary and unwelcoming when you're young and rootless. I found my place, and my people, and remembered that this was home. For Christmas lunch in 2000, the first Christmas after my not-yet wife and I moved into our Stoke Newington flat, we had a winter picnic at Highbury Fields – the blueprint for every family Christmas since. Although we don't always picnic; it's in December, for goodness' sake. We'd been a couple several years by then, but that meal, that moment, was, as I say, the beginning of our family life together – marriage, children, our home; the seed was planted that cold afternoon, posh Christmas trees glowing in the windows of the tall, beautiful houses.

By the time I got to Highbury Fields parkrun in 2015, we – my wife, our two kids and I – all lived in the house we're in now, which is about a mile away from Highbury; a nice warm-up run's distance. Twenty-one-year-old me, twenty-one years before, would have had his mind comprehensively blown by the idea that I'd be living nearby with my family, clowning for a living, and that I'd be mooching down there on a Saturday morning . . . for a *run*!

As you probably know by now, I took a very solitary route into running, so parkrun was a paradigm shift for me – a bunch of my running peers, in the same place, doing the same thing. For the uninitiated, a parkrun is a five-kilometre run on a Saturday morning at the same time every week, with volunteer marshals setting you up and starting you off around a clearly laid out course, and your result emailed to you afterwards. You don't have to book or pay; you just register, print off a barcode, turn up and run. It's beautiful. And there I was. At this rate, I was going to have to admit that I was a runner.

But that's the wonderful thing about parkrun – the organisation's concept of what a runner is chimes completely with mine: a runner is not necessarily an athlete, or a speed freak, or a very-serious-faced person with all the right gear and not an ounce of body fat. A runner is simply someone who runs.

Highbury Fields parkrun starts up a slight hill through the tree-lined boulevard next to the biggest, most open patch of grass – field, I suppose I should say – turns left and loops it, dropping down the hill again on the other side. This circuit is slightly less than a kilometre, so you run round five times, then motor up the slope one last, sixth time. I was amazed how quickly, once tired, I could get confused about how many times I'd been round, and on future visits I would take to counting off the laps on my fingers, also relying on which songs I'd heard on my running playlist to tell me how far I'd come – or not.

The other wonderful thing about a parkrun – for me, at least – is how fast it makes you go. The other people there gee me up to a great pace at the start, and then it's just a question of holding on – and that's where the songs come in. When you really need a running song, you're looking for a perfect, almost impossible blend: a tune that makes you run harder and faster than you knew you could, while simultaneously distracting you from the task at hand. That first parkrun, I kept having to skip tracks that weren't helping me round – these days I have a playlist called Parkrun Bangers that's carefully curated for the purpose – but then, as I rounded the playground and gym at the south, downhill end of Highbury Fields for something like the fourth time and headed back up the hill, Missy Elliott's 'Can't Stop' played.

What a tune; more than a tune – a statement of intent. A huge, syncopated cascade of brass chords kicks things off, then, while you're still catching your breath, a single-note, processed bassline grabs you by the back of the head and propels you into the song. That day, it was a quintessential example of the perfect, almost impossible blend; I simultaneously started running faster and forgot I was running at all.

Then Missy Elliot's rap begins. That first parkrun, which was some time after I'd heard it on the radio, I belatedly heeded Lauren Laverne's caveat. Missy E was not talking about running. This is a song about sex, and it's much too muscular for hints and double entendres; it's powerful, honest and fantastic, and that day it hugely helped with my run – and in a far less knowing and ironic way than that Johnny Bristol cut.

What can I say? It's a banger.

So my love of parkrun was sealed and set, and my time was good. I had a mild sense of embarrassment among the other runners once I was done, based on decorum, but they didn't know what I'd been listening to, right? It wasn't like I'd been running round with a dirty magazine . . . They seemed like a nice bunch of people, and it might have been a good chance to mingle, but I didn't catch anyone's eye.

I think I just looked a bit too hungry.

These days, if I can get to a local parkrun, I tend to favour Hackney Marshes, which is significantly further away from my house. I tell myself it's because Highbury's hill and five-plus laps are a bit much, but, if I'm honest, I don't think that's quite it. I love Highbury Fields parkrun; in fact, I've loved every parkrun I've ever been to, and I've taken part in them all over Britain; I would happily do any one of them every Saturday. But despite being a short walk from the rich wonders – and the ups and downs – of Islington, I live happily in flat Hackney. For all its local loveliness, for better or worse, Highbury Fields is still the dream – a place for firsts, for challenges, for the life I nearly have. If I went there every Saturday, where would I go when I wanted to go somewhere special?

Another tune like this: 'Gett Off' by Prince. Filth with an enormous backbeat.

Another run like this: I live really near Finsbury Park, which has a great parkrun, but I've only ever done it once. No one knows why.

15. HITTING THE BERLIN WALL
Germany 2015

I am a surprisingly nippy runner.

I have a slightly awkward, rolling-shouldered gait – I don't look like an athlete, because I've never been one. Although I'm no longer a big, chubby fellow, I spent so much of my life as one that it defines my personality in lots of ways. What can I say . . . I'm jolly. But I've got a fair turn of speed – over distance, at least. It's innate, not looked-for, trained or encouraged at all in my younger days. During Games at school, I would be picked last for everything, every time – and that was when I hadn't come up with some ingenious way to skip the lesson altogether. Cross-country running was just a punishment in those days. Occasionally, at school, there would be a flash of my natural running disposition – a surprising win in a chase in a playground game, a couple of tortoise–hare moments on sports day when I could get all the way round the track once or twice without slowing down or stopping – but basically, no one knew – and I'm including myself here. I was lardy and inert, and that worked for me.

When I got into running, I did it all in my own time and in my own way. It was literally years, and several marathons and half marathons, before I knew anything about the mechanics of pacing and training – I didn't want to think about it, in case it spoiled this lovely new, not-overly-cerebral experience I'd found. Naive Running Me had one pace – I ran out of the door fast, like I was chasing a bus, and kept it up for as long as I could. I didn't like stopping or even turning – like a clockwork toy.

Gradually, I found a way to stretch this attitude over ten, thirteen, twenty-six miles. Always for charity, always listening to music, I was nevertheless really *running* these things. Even more gradually, I began to find out what it all meant – times, PBs, going off too fast. It all felt like nothing to do with me.

From where I am now, heading for fifty, it's galling to see the offhand way I got my fastest times in those days. Remember me doing the Royal Parks Half Marathon and skipping round in less than an hour and a half? I wasn't even thinking about it. If I had been, could I have even done it that fast? I certainly haven't repeated it since; I had just achieved my PB before knowing it stood for

Personal Best, let alone that it was a thing. When my friend explained what it all meant – my time, my potential – I was like (cartoon-bewildered-idiot voice): '*Ungh?!*' But a seed was planted.

From that moment on, I started chipping away at my own innocence. I started going into events with an idea of what I should be able to do, even choosing events with a personal achievement in mind. It was the right way to go – my lack of self-awareness couldn't last forever; as a runner I was growing up. Plus, not incidentally, the guilt I felt about the narcissism of challenging myself in this way meant that I worked extra hard at the fundraising. Every marathon I did to get a good time raised thousands for Parkinson's UK.

But it was a wobbly time. There would be no more accidental successes. As you know, I did get under three and a quarter hours in foggy York, with the help of Goths and mistakes – but, of course, that didn't slake my thirst at all; I was just hungry for the next achievement. I was really fit for the London Marathon in 2015, and I thought I could get my fastest time, maybe even go under three hours and ten minutes, but – horror of horrors – my headphones broke after about ten miles, and though I hammered on, I tired just a little, and got a time that disappointed me. It disappointed me then, anyway; I'd give my right arm for it now.

Along with a natural loss of innocence as I matured as

a runner, there was sometimes a loss of focus on *why* I ran. I run for the joy of it – I don't have to prove anything, to myself or anyone else. And I run to spend time listening to music. There was nothing I could do about those headphones breaking, but what happened, music-wise, in my next marathon tells a different story.

I had set my sights on Berlin. Less than six months after London, the Berlin Marathon is another of the World Marathon Majors, the six international big-city marathons one is encouraged to collect – although three are in America, which is a bit of a cheek. Berlin is a famously fast course. I could roll my fitness over to this alterno-London – 40,000 people slicing through the heart of a major European city, but flatter, with working headphones – and get my three-ten after all.

Parkinson's UK got me a place in the race. They even very kindly advanced me a little money for a plane ticket and a hotel room, and I vowed to make it count. I would be in and out of Germany, speedily and cheaply, medal on my chest, PB in my back pocket, bish-bash-bosh. I booked my plane ticket really early, so it was super cheap; I'd be in town for twenty-four hours – teatime on Saturday till teatime on Sunday; I found a surprisingly reasonable-value hotel room not far from the start.

I trained hard and steadily all summer, and every time I ran, I'd post a link to my fundraising page. I took a bucket for donations to all my gigs and stood by the door at the end. People were generous, and really lovely about it, too.

But when the final race information came through, there was a problem. I had to pick up my running number from the pre-marathon expo before it finished on the night before the marathon, and I wasn't going to be in town in time. *Gah!* I tried to change my flight, but the most cost-effective way to fix this was to book a completely different, still bargain-priced earlier one. In the event, I was still nearly late – the old airport where the expo takes place is enormous, along a commensurately enormous road, and just the walk from the nearest S-Bahn train station took me an hour. I was so stressed out.

Thankfully, the mighty Mickey D was there, and he talked me down. Mickey D is an Australian comedian, runner and force of nature. The positive energy off him is a tonic; he had run the London Marathon that year too, and we'd toured in Norway just afterwards, which was an amazing trip – that time we *did* go to Bergen. I didn't see much of him at all in Berlin, but the couple of moments when I did catch up with him he saved the day. Here he was at the expo, with a grin, a raised eyebrow and a positive attitude to this adventure that was entirely the opposite of my own; my head was down and I was freaking out. Plus, he had the internet on his iPad, which helped with problem number two: I had been placed in a starting pen way back in the funnel, the pre-start line stretch of course where they kettle all the runners before the race, according to how fast they are likely to run. I had to convince a steward to move me up the pack, based on that speedy time I'd achieved in the Yorkshire Marathon. Reasonably, but stressfully, the steward didn't believe me – so, Mickey D got the race results up on screen, and I got a starting spot much nearer the actual start line after all. Phew!

I took my leave of Mickey D and headed off in search of problems three and four.

My hotel, it turned out, was in the suburbs. The location was gorgeous, but it wasn't what I'd planned. I don't quite know what went wrong, but I think I mixed up a spot in the city centre with a district with the same name. In London terms, I thought I was staying on Oxford Street – but my hotel turned out to be in Oxford. Geographically, this is an exaggeration, but not much of one; I was going to have to get up *early* in the morning to get a train into town and reach the start on time.

Never mind. I'd get an early night – once I'd sorted everything out, that is. I paced back and forth in my hotel room, fiddling with safety pins, plasters, carbohydrate gels, shoelaces; I knew I was in a totally unhelpful tizz, but I couldn't shake it. I should have put some music on, but I just rattled around in my silent suite. Ah well – the same time the next day I'd be home and it would be all over. In fact, best to check in for the return flight now.

I got on my own internet this time and tried to check in. It wouldn't work for some reason; I tried a few times, a couple of different ways, emailed Customer Service . . . Never mind – I'd sort it out when I got to the airport. *Midnight!* Go to bed, go to bed, go to bed . . .

I made the early train, reached the starting area and found the toilet before the queue got really long. It was shaping up to be a nice day – sunny, still and cool. The starting area for the Berlin Marathon is also the finishing area – the course is one big loop of the city – so knowing what the hell was going on and where I was supposed to be at the finish was one less thing to worry about; I would be back here.

Into the pens. Serious runners! Where was Mickey D? Never mind. *Boom!* Balloons into the sky and off we went. It felt good to be running; I could listen to some music and shut the voice in my head up at last.

What songs played in those first minutes of the run? I have no memory of them at all. I know, it was years ago, but I would normally remember, and I'm prepared to bet that if you'd asked me later that day I still wouldn't have known.

The pace felt good – steady, not too fast; *I could keep this up for hours,* I thought. Between us, let me admit now that I was wrong about that. I was going . . . quickly. I was basically running as fast as I could – with twenty-five miles to go. But I felt OK. Everyone tends to go off a bit fast in a marathon, and I maintained that speed for a long time.

I wasn't enjoying it, though. Lots of bland, flat roads. Another nondescript junction, a slight turn, another bland, flat road. No one in fancy dress, no balloons, no crowds of either spectators or charity supporters on the sidelines. A much drier atmosphere than London – or Yorkshire. At one point another runner took me by both shoulders and moved me out of his way. What's that all about? *At least I have my music* is what I should have thought – but no. It still wasn't going in; my ears were closed.

Two super-fit Finnish girls were running together, their names printed in pink on their grey Lycra shorts, a pha-lanx of guys running along behind them. Coincidence? Or bum-watching? Seedy if the latter – I wanted nothing to do with it, but the pace I had to make to get past them all . . . Wow. Still – three-ten's the goal, right? Onwards!

It stayed sunny and still, but it wasn't cool. I was get-ting hot – and thirsty. There were kilometre markers but no mile ones – again, totally reasonable, but I could have done with a little, low-key imperial measurement every now and again. If we're only counting this in kilometres . . . well, there are over forty-two of those to deal with, and that's a lot, particularly when the markers seem to be getting further and further apart.

I had a drink from a water station. The water was in a little paper cup and I had to stop running to drink it. Stopping shook me to the very core – I hate breaking stride, with superstitious fervour – but I started off again. I had now run over twenty miles – which is, what? Fifty, sixty kilometres? – at fierce pace and I was feeling it. I was flagging; my ability to run fading, and my ability to do maths gone. I had another drink, and a walk, and this time I did not start running again.

I'd got a long way at a good speed – actually forty kilometres, which is plenty – but none of that matters if you can't take it home. Now I was walking and thinking, *Forget it*. Occasionally, I'd break into a half-arsed jog, but I just hated myself for that. As we rounded the corner to see the Brandenburg Gate, metres from the finish line, a passing runner said in English, 'Running for charity, eh?' and I felt deeply belittled. We won't ever know if he meant it in a patronising way – I was certainly in a foul enough mood to be projecting the negativity I felt – but I didn't like it.

And still not one song had got through to me – my headphones were working, but I heeded them not; no power rock had jolted me back into action; no repetitive beats had sparked dance-y joy in me; no lyrics had juxtaposed ridiculously with what I was up to.

I crossed the finish line. It was over. I had thrown away the opportunity to run an amazing marathon but done quite enough to feel entirely broken, and I was absolutely livid with myself for getting a time that was actually faster than any of the many marathons I would run between 2017 and 2020. I took my headphones out, for all the good they had done me. How far outside my mental comfort zone I had strayed.

Each finisher was handed a yellow plastic poncho and gently herded towards the pretty, sunny rose garden where our bags waited for us. No one spoke, we just drifted forwards, rustling. Speakers played uplifting music. At that moment, seconds after I'd finished, the song that came on was 'Hero' by Family of the Year – you might know it from the soundtrack to the film *Boyhood*. It's absolutely beautiful – sparkling acoustic guitar picking and sweetly sung, diary-like lyrics, gently opening out to a country-and-westernish, folky pulse. The sound of a little boy under a big sky.

It is not, however, celebratory. It's lovely, but heartbreaking. It's about *not* being a hero; it's about simply soldiering on. It was too much for me. Out loud, I said, 'Come on!', and I chuckled, trying to front it out, but I had a little cry, and oh, my heart . . . Music had found and helped me at last.

Then I found two things: free steins of Erdinger Alkoholfrei, which is the best non-alcoholic beer there is, as well as being an entirely healthy isotonic sports drink – according to Germans at least – and Mickey D, smile, eyebrow and good spirits in place, to remind me of my sense of humour, my smile, and joy in general. He'd run the same marathon as me, yet been on an entirely different journey. But what did it matter now? We'd both finished it, and so had all those other people. Thousands of stories faded into one. The medals, after all, were the same. Also, he lent me a towel so I could change my pants right there in the middle of the park.

So, Berlin was not the marathon for me. The weekend had a bad energy from beginning to end. I'll never know if that's why I ran a poor race, or whether I'd have run the same one on a happier day, but I'm glad of that cathartic song now; it really drew the sting.

Was that the end of the story? No. I hotfooted it to the airport where an old guy who worked for British Airways, ignoring my tear-streaked cheeks and hard-won medal, wouldn't let me check in for my plane home because I hadn't taken the outbound one that I'd booked at the same time – and instead charged me hundreds of pounds for a new seat on the very same flight.

It was a good trip.

Another tune like this: Newton Faulkner's 'Dream Catch Me' is another folk-inflected, slightly wistful slice of pop that I wouldn't think had much to do with me – except I can't sing along to it without having a little cry.

Another run like this: I don't want to speak ill of marathons I haven't done, but a couple of other runners I've met have told me very similar stories to this one of mine, about Paris and Amsterdam respectively. Maybe we all got too excited, anticipating the thrill of a hip, European city, forgetting for a moment what our primary purpose there would be – i.e. not so much hanging with the cool kids checking out the scene as simply running along city streets for hours. In kilometres. So many kilometres.

16. RUNNING UP THIS HILL
Dale Head 2016

And then there was the time I listened to Kate Bush's 'Running Up That Hill' while I ran up a hill.

In August 2016, Steve Lamacq's show on BBC Radio 6 Music ran a 'World Cup' of running songs. This was, as you will easily surmise, right up my street – theoretically, at least – and as a friend of Steve's and the show, I was lucky enough to be able to get involved. I went to the studio for the initial draw – I suppose there must have been sixteen songs – and then went all round Britain to try some of them out on the ground.

They were some wonderful runs. And don't worry, the BBC wasn't blowing cash on this; the 'tournament' conveniently – cleverly? – fell on a week when I was travelling from the Edinburgh Festival Fringe to the Green Man Festival in South Wales, stopping off for a stolen, momentary holiday in the Lake District with my family between the two.

Plus, thank goodness, the weather was glorious. We only had one full day in the Lakes, staying in Seatoller in Borrowdale, and the chances of rain were very high indeed – we were within strolling distance of the very wettest places in England. Had it rained, the little holiday would have been . . . disappointing. As it was, the day included a family walk up one of the area's most beautiful mountains, a swim in a limpid river pool – although I skipped this bit to talk on the radio and my wife skipped it because it was so blimmin' cold – and, for me, before breakfast, a run.

I'm not a run-at-dawn guy. When I first got into running, I tried very hard to be; I distinctly remember being out one winter morning, during my first year of running, in complete darkness and with the temperature at minus six – but it's not for me. It's a fact that running is good for one's mental health; I think part of that is the time it requires you to spend with yourself, doing this, and only this. It creates a mindful, meditative space that I, for one, would never have otherwise found – so, ways to cheat that time – running before everyone else gets up, running in a gym, interval training to trick your body into fast improvement – don't work for me. I need to take the time, in my own time, and commit to the run.

Plus, as I found on that early run in Suffolk, my bowels

won't let me get away with it. If I get up at 6.45 a.m. and head out for a run at 7, I will need to be running into a bathroom at 7.15. Ideally, a bathroom with something to read in it. I think you probably get what I'm saying here.

Don't worry, this story doesn't end with me soiling myself in the Cumbrian fells; I'm just saying I'm not a run-at-dawn guy. But that August morning, I knew that I had to be up in the heights running and recording and down again before 8 a.m. My idea was to run up Dale Head because you can park part way up, at Honister Pass, and be at the top in not much more than a mile, but it's still a significant peak with a stunning surprise view at the summit.

I have the wherewithal to record myself talking while I run, owing to Paul Tonkinson's and my podcast. Working out how to record ourselves chatting while we run was a challenge, but once we'd cracked the code it was pretty straightforward – the biggest ongoing difficulty is running while wearing a McDonald's drive-thru-style headset microphone. In this instance, I had the added issue of having to talk to myself, but if we're honest, it wasn't that much of a problem. Of course, running alone and talking to myself lacked the fun, inspiration and genuine dialogue I get – and need – when podcasting with Paul, but living through even the most solitary, mundane moments of my life as if I'm in front of a large, apprecia-tive audience pretty much sums up what it's like in my head; describing my adventure out loud wasn't going to be a stretch. If I didn't do the jobs I do, I don't know what I'd do with myself.

And although I was completely, excitingly alone that morning, I was working. I knew that Alison, the producer, was in on the plan and relying on me to send her something she could use. I realised that, without really talking about it, we both had this comedy postcard-style mental image of me in the rain, under a dripping cagoule hood, pretty miserable, with only a few hardy mountain sheep for company. But that was not how it turned out at all.

I had chosen the moment I would actually start running for purely logistical reasons – I'd allowed myself enough time to get up to the top, down to the car again and be back at the hotel in time for breakfast. So I couldn't believe my luck when this run revealed itself to be what it really was – a religiously fantastic sunrise run. With only a few hardy mountain sheep for company.

The path from the road at Honister Pass to the top of Dale Head is direct but demoralising – a constant climb, with the end always out of sight. It's a bit of a pain to walk up but better to run. This wasn't my first time going up a fell in my trainers, but I hadn't done it much – I still haven't. I think it's great; being on an actual mountain changes the rules in a really empowering way. If you run up a city street that's a hill, your body doesn't even register it as a hill – you just feel rough and heavy and useless.

Psychologically, I find a slight incline can actually be tougher than a steep escarpment; on the mountainside you know where you are and you remember your gears – go as slow as you like, take your time, this is a *climb*! Plus, this is wild country, with rocks, mud, heather and scree – every step is a careful choice; you can't help but pace yourself. In the Lake District I know that if I run slow and steady I can get right to the top, so by goodness I slow it down.

I ran a little way to be sure I could, then started my recorder. The running songs World Cup had actually thrown the twisted sophistry of my own running music choices into stark relief. First of all, my playlist choices are always based on instrumental music first and foremost; euphoric melodies and chords, propulsive basslines and beats already feel pretty literal to me. Every now and again in life I'm reminded how important the words being sung are – of course they are! I've learned this over time, and I appreciate good lyrics, but that's just not where my musical mind starts from. Secondly, I resist the obvious; if something is on the nose – which is by no means always a bad thing – I reject it.

The World Cup of running songs was full of songs about running!

Funnily enough, famous songs that refer to running are never about actual running. The Spencer Davis Group's 'Keep on Running' is more about stalkiness. Bryan Adams'

'Run to You' is about adultery. Bruce Springsteen's 'Born to Run' is about rebellion and escape – he's on a motorbike, for goodness' sake. Probably the most famous literal running tune is Vangelis' theme from *Chariots of Fire* – but of course, that's instrumental.

So, no two ways about it, I was resistant to considering 'Running Up That Hill' as a running song as I ran up that hill listening to it. What's it about? Grown-up relationships, gender roles and the great slog of life, I suppose. The original title was 'A Deal with God', but the record company advised Kate Bush to change it because Americans can be funny about that kind of thing. I can't help thinking that if it had been called that, despite the chorus being exactly the same, it might not have made the list.

But Kate Bush knows what she's doing. The relentless chug of the one-note bassline of the song is the perfect aural representation of life as a tough yet subtly beautiful never-ending run uphill. I had to concede this, and I enjoyed listening to it, and the song went on to win the Cup.

It is a bit of a downer, though.

I was halfway through my ascent and I'd recorded more than enough for my brief feature, so I switched my little machine off. To my right, over the black silhouette of the mighty Helvellyn range, the sun rose and the world switched from blue to gold. I plodded on towards the top. Dale Head is crowned with a mighty cairn, taller than a person, so eventually, with just a hundred yards or so to go, you see it, beckoning you on. But it is only when you actually reach the peak that the mountain reveals its spectacular secret. The long, curving fell you've come to know on your climb ends right there – within a foot or two of the cairn the land drops away almost vertically and, instead, rolled out in front of you, far below, is a stunningly beautiful valley. This is Newlands, the dale you're at the head of – and beyond it, to the north, you see the angular, grey-purple foothills, flanks and pointy top of Skiddaw, the closest thing to a child's drawing of a mountain in the whole of the Lake District.

My broadcasting mission complete, the mountain conquered at a run, I reached this point just as the sideways sunlight spread across this splendid spot, showing it at its not inconsiderable best. It was ecstasy. Another dawn mountaineer walked by – the first other human I'd seen so far that day – and I waved hello. I could have hugged him. Although I would have been sweaty and he would have been scared.

I turned left and ran a little further along the ridge towards the next peak, Hindscarth. Now that I was no longer climbing, I felt as though I could run all day, out into this incredible view to the west. The tunes I was listening to sounded like – no, they *were* – the best tunes in the world; long, rhythmic, spacious rock and dance anthems from my younger days. But . . . breakfast. I turned back, ran past the cairn, taking one last look at Newlands and all the mountains around, now completely bathed in sunlight, and headed back down the hill. At this moment, by chance, my actual, personal number-one running tune played – 'Space Shanty' by Leftfield, hitting the ground with floor-filling rhythms and figures from the start, but constantly inventive, with as much for your head to roll with as your hips – cleverer and less harsh-sounding than the hardest techno I listen to, but with all the oomph intact. It's relentless – the kick-drum beat, the pumping octave bassline, the rotating organ arpeggio; every new detail satisfying and repetitive in its own right, but all of them working together to become something spectacular, like the shiny cogs and springs of a priceless antique clock. But from the 1990s.

Even in a car park this song would make me feel like I was flying at a thousand miles an hour; hearing it during this descent, with the highest, most impressive countryside in England spread out before me, was transcendent.

Then I tripped, stumbled and very nearly *did* go flying at a thousand miles an hour. The momentum, going down an incline like that, at that pace, is something else – you're not stopping, or even slowing down; if you stumble, you're either going to get your feet back underneath you and run on or you're going to dive down the mountainside instead. Suddenly, the very real possibility of a broken tooth or ankle brought me back down to earth – but it was for the best. Like a string on a kite, I needed a little something to connect this incredible high to the ground below. I ran on – *nearly* as fast – down to the car, the village, breakfast and a beautiful day that had barely begun.

Another tune like this: Almost any other Leftfield. Their 'Phat Planet' – the bass-heavy stomp that, if you're my age, you might remember from an old Guinness advert – is a massive running tune, guaranteed to make you go a little bit faster.

Another run like this: Pen y Fan in the Brecon Beacons or Salisbury Crags in Edinburgh both reveal incredible views at their summits. Be sure to stop running on arrival if you don't want your descent to be quicker than intended.

17. I DON'T HAVE FAVOURITES
Regent's Canal 2016

So many of these stories invoke high adventure – or at least marathons and the seaside – that I think it's important to spend a moment with the bread and butter of my running, the kind of bimble I've done hundreds of times, and doubtless take for granted, but nevertheless really look forward to, and miss when I'm not able to do.

Between getting my regular run up to seven miles and starting to record Running Commentary, my podcast with Paul Tonkinson – I may have mentioned it – I ran seven miles three times a week, steadily and stolidly, for about five years. This was 2010–2015-ish. I collected a soul-massaging playlist of wonderful songs, rotating them regularly on my little clip-iPod. I developed routes from my house – one each to the north, south, east and west, roughly – and if I wasn't away somewhere I'd run one of those. I'd decide which it was to be the night before, or just before, over coffee; by then I'd know what I felt like doing – even if it meant reversing the decision of the previous bedtime.

Of course, it made no odds which route I took – I suppose that might seem to make the decision harder; might as well toss a coin – but I always enjoyed the clarity. I'd feel like I'd just seen *that* park, but I was just in the mood for *that* body of water . . . This stuff doesn't really matter, but it's important to me. Each route is a once-round loop, the four of them hardly intersect and they all have different characters – the fast there-and-back, the one that visits all my local parks and lakes, the really spacious one . . . I am so lucky to have such choice at my feet, particularly as every mile of every run features new and different scenery and stuff to see. I'm scared of getting bored, and I used to worry that, after a while, this bunch of routes would lose their flavour, like chewing gum you've had in your mouth for a bit too long. Instead, they became lenses through which I could watch the weather and the seasons. The paths, the turns, the buildings – they're always the same; but the sky, the greenery, the surface of the water, the way the air feels – they're never the same twice.

I might have predicted this if I hadn't had unexamined prejudices about the town and the country. A country home with a beautiful view – actually, not necessarily beautiful, just a view, a window out onto the natural world – will always show you something different. Change is constant, and, if anything, when some part of it *does* look the same twice, you welcome it. I stayed in a house in Sweden years ago, and the evening I arrived, the creek behind it was like a mirror, reflecting the trees beyond. 'How lovely,' I thought, and looked forward to seeing it again the next day – but the next day the creek rippled in the wind, and the next day it rained . . . and in the end, I never saw that reflection again. If I'd been there long enough to witness the effect once more, I would have welcomed it like an old friend.

It was running that taught me that it's just the same in a town, and that, over time, those small, welcome waves of familiarity resolve into the seasons – that tree is where the biggest, shiniest conkers fall in the autumn; that stretch of the canal is where you could well see daffodils and big fluffy cygnets in spring; that bit of path will be a treacherous mudbath from November to March, unless there's been some really dry weather. And so on.

My running playlist weaves through this mental map like a double-helix; sometimes a song will bring new emotional colour to a street I've pounded a hundred times; sometimes the weather will bring new meaning to a tune I've been listening to for decades. My virtual DJ, knowing nothing of my environment, provides the perfect counterpoint to it.

I still run those routes, but these days I mix things up a lot more – longer runs, shorter, faster, runs with Paul, with my wife – plus my life is a tour, so there are, and always have been, forays into other areas. Meanwhile my well of songs is deeper than ever, and because of those chatty trots I run with music less of the time, so individual tracks pop up with far less regularity. Now, when I get my headphones on and do one of the compass-based seven-milers out of my front door, it always feels like comfort food – revisiting a classic; if I hear a tune that I've been enjoying since my earliest runs while I'm out there, that's even better.

And I think, out of those four routes, I have a favourite. No – favourite is too strong; it's just my go-to run – the 'control' other runs can be compared to. Why has it become my most-used route, the run I fall back on? Let's take a look and see.

I start south, with the couple of hundred yards to pretty Newington Green – busy, a roundabout essentially, but also a well-used little park bounded by tall trees and old, interesting buildings. It's a faffy start, hard to get into a rhythm, I suppose, and a situation exacerbated by the fact that my mus

ic player often cu

ts out quite irrita

tingly when I firs

t turn it on. But it gets over itself and starts playing

steadily around the point where I pick up the broad pavement of Mildmay Park, dropping out of the green south towards De Beauvoir Town, creating a nice sense of 'warm-up completed, proper run just beginning'. And here starts a big, simple part of this run's attraction: this first half mile or so is ever so slightly downhill – just enough to make me feel a teensy bit faster and fitter than I actually am.

Once that effect has worn off, my pace is set and the unimaginative machine that is my body will not change it. Plus I've arrived in the broad, leafy streets of De Beauvoir Town, which is just as lush as it sounds. From there I pass through Haggerston, which is far less rough than it sounds, with a park, a pub, a church, a nice parade of shops and, come to think of it, a raft of happy memories – a Halloween party in the hall there where I performed my one-man cover version of Warren Zevon's 'Werewolves of London'; bumping into an old friend and band-mate from school propping up the bar in said pub; getting some good news about, of all things, a nursing home for my dad while I was in that park. Haggerston, it turns out, is an auspicious spot.

It seems like this run is already onto a winner, but only now do we get to what I think of as the heart of the thing: the canal.

It's the Regent's Canal, which runs from Paddington to Limehouse Basin. About three songs into my run I get onto the towpath next to the bridge that gives the Bridge Academy school its name, and turn right – west, heading for Angel, another song-and-a-half away. The Bridge Academy is an incredible bit of architecture: several curved floors of school stuff – classrooms, laboratories, etc. – ranged around a central atrium then covered over on the diagonal with a huge, sloping, clear roof. There are a lot of interesting buildings like this along the south side of the canal. There's the refurbished and repurposed Gainsborough film studios, there are several floors of flats behind a living wall of gravity-defying foliage, an old, square Victorian chimney which must have been a nightmare to build, and more. I pass under numerous little brick bridges and past a couple of gorgeous locks, still well used; I often see narrowboats going through the rigmarole of negotiating them, and once helped a brusque young woman get a lock gate open. She would have *loved* to have not needed my help – quite right, too – and I had to really prove my worth, using every ounce of my strength and, let's face it, greater weight to get the thing moving. It was a nice moment; nary a smile shared, but communion nonetheless.

Just once, as I trotted along this stretch, there was a torrential downpour. For a moment, I sheltered under the dark arch of one of those brick bridges. Peering through the grey curtain of the rain, I could see a couple of people silhouetted sheltering under the next bridge – and the bridge after that. It was beautiful. I ran on; after all, you can't wait for the rain to stop – it might never happen.

I've seen the towpath in all weathers, and I've learned to love the fact that when the weather's nice, it's busy. I've been out along there in weekend sunshine, dodging bikes, circumnavigating families, waiting out of the way as dogs and oldsters, and oldsters with their dogs, make their way past. It really breaks up one's rhythm, but I say to myself, *Don't wish the sunlight and society away; soon enough, you'll be back here on a miserable Monday morning in November – and you'll have it all to yourself.* And soon enough I always do.

Amazingly, after a gorgeous lock-keeper's cottage and broad turning area for the boats, the canal goes completely underground for several hundred yards at Angel. What a thing it would have been, back in the day, to send your ponies up over the hill and get through the tunnel by lying on your back on the roof of your barge and moving it by walking your feet along the ceiling – that's how they did it! What a feeling, when you're walking on the ceiling, as Lionel Richie once so nearly sang.

If you look straight ahead through the dark mouth of the tunnel at just the right moment, you can see the daylight at the other end, beyond the Caledonian Road, towards King's Cross – another run for another day. I climb steeply right and up the road to Angel, the nearest shopping hub and mall to my home, and head right up

Upper Street – a gorgeous, posh street of fancy restaurants and chi-chi shops, another repository of fun memories. Brilliantly, it's also the A1 – if I stay on this road and just keep on going, it will take me to York, Newcastle and Edinburgh. I cross at Highbury Corner and go round the long side of Highbury Fields, a gentler slope but a small pull nonetheless, the 'hill' in my original three-mile run. And the site of my first, Missy Elliott-spiced parkrun. And that Christmas picnic with my not-yet wife. So many memories.

From Highbury Fields I pass between the clock tower and the church to the mini high street known as Highbury Barn, the heart of the original village on this spot. Apparently the barn was a place where people, led by the twinkling lights at the top of the hill, used to come to party – the original ravers. The Highbury Barn pub sits in the middle of the scene now, keeping the name and the dream alive. It's a brief but busy stretch, which is a challenge as I have to hop in and out of the road to avoid either vehicles or pedestrians. Then hard right – on a blind corner where I've given people coming the other way a terrible fright more than once ... sorry, guys – down the hill again to the point where my beloved, local Clissold Park meets Green Lanes. I'm home now, but I loop the park once to see who's about and make up the numbers, distance-wise, before the half mile back to my house.

Looking at it like this, I now realise that this run is absolutely riddled with memory – running and otherwise. It's a living, walk-in map of my day-to-day life, my running history and all the great moments of my life with my wife and my family. Maybe that's why it's my favourite – and maybe favourite isn't too strong a word after all.

It also goes right past the bank. 'Can I help you with anything in particular, sir?' 'No thanks, just making a deposit.' The friendly staff can almost always hide the relief they feel at not having to interact with the sweaty, huffing man any more than this.

So, there you have it. If you want to cut right to the essence of my running, you could do worse than run fast along the Regent's Canal towpath between the Rosemary Branch and the Narrowboat pubs on a cold, grey, autumn morning, not windy or wet, and listen to 'Moments' by Kidnap Kid, featuring Leo Stannard – mournful yet propulsive, dancey but lyrical; a delicate, dampened piano figure over repetitive beats, under a lyric about the elusive magic of feeling without thinking, and about memories. It's got everything I love in a slice of running music: pace, spacious production and a wistful blend of hope and sadness.

I heard it when I was down there once, on a run like that, and, in among all those other times, all those other adventures, I remember it well; as well as if some part of me were still down there. And I think, in a way, it probably still is.

Another tune like this: Interesting production, with thoughtful use of acoustic instruments over dancey beats and samples, under a beautifully sung lyric, can also be found on 'Nightlite' by Bonobo, featuring Bajka.

Another run like this: Victorian engineering that takes you through cathartic greenery near my house can also be found on the Parkland Walk, the lovely wooded disused railway that runs from Finsbury Park to Highgate.

18. SHAKEDOWN TIME

Hackney Marshes 2017

You've got to love a parkrun.

I certainly do; I get to one whenever I can. I've got better and better at turning off that alarm and getting up and out on a Saturday, and I've taken to factoring new parkruns into my touring schedule.

Parkrun wouldn't exist without the internet, of course – as a social hub for participants and as a place to organise events, share course information, results and news. It's the internet working at its very best in fact, combining, as it does, unselfish democracy, positive communication and a good, solid link to something that happens outside in real life. The social vibe is palpable at the events. Each parkrun has its own community – regulars who run every week, and a floating rota of volunteers coming together to make it happen – but they welcome newbies and visitors with open arms and make it absolutely clear that this is a run, not a race; every participant has equal agency, from the person walking their dog round and taking their time to the would-be Olympic youth streaking round in not much more than fifteen minutes, via everyone in between.

I've been to parkruns all over Britain. Visiting a new one is such a good bet, because they're all great, but they're not all the same; well, in simple terms, they are – exactly the same – but each one has its own distinct geography and character. Kind of like episodes of *Columbo*. I'm certainly not the only parkrun tourist out there, but most of the people I meet are very loyal to one event, local to them, and will often tell me in no uncertain terms that theirs is the best one.

Which, in a way, is true.

There's a brilliant balance to this 'one for all, all for one' spirit. I feel very happy going to a different run every Saturday, but I also love coming home to Hackney Marshes parkrun, and there's no contradiction in this, just as there's no contradiction in the fact that, despite a parkrun avowedly not being a race, there will be plenty of people there racing – the point is that it's your run, and, as long as you respect the form, and the space you're in, that can mean whatever you want it to mean.

My dad and my brother were always sporty and competitive, while my mum opted out and I was too little to be any good, so as a youngster I never enjoyed sporty games. As a result, I never built a relationship with sociable competitiveness the way some other people do. It always feels harsh to me, even though I know how positive – and affectionate – it is for some people. Also – confession alert – it's not that I don't like to win; I do! I only really enjoy things I'm good at, and in all aspects of life I have a tendency to either have a proper go at excelling, or give up completely. Unimaginative of me, really, but there it is. And I'll always express myself in terms of laughs and self-deprecation; I am ashamed of my own competitive spirit, and other people's competitive natures make me cross. This, after a fair few years of running solo, was where parkrun came in. At a parkrun I can happily race with strangers – because it's not a race. And that's not hypocrisy; that indirectness makes it so much clearer that keying off other people is just a way of racing the only person I'm ever really racing against – myself.

It still took some getting used to. It turns out that, among people who are in the habit of running a given distance as fast as they can, running even faster right at the end is a thing. Who knew?! Everyone, probably. But I didn't. At 4,900 metres into a 5,000-metre race – sorry, *run* – I will already definitely be going literally as fast as I can. So, the first few times that I experienced guys suddenly appearing around my shoulders and whipping over the line in the last few moments of a parkrun, I took it as a personal affront. Luckily I was too shy and polite to say

make you feel as rough as the bottom of a birdcage. The enjoyment isn't so much intangible as imaginary.

And yet . . . and yet.

The joy of knowing that all those strangers made the same choice as me to be there at the start line fills my heart with a sense of human kinship. As soon as the run is over, there is something we can all share, and even if that's expressed through nothing more than a nod or a handshake, it gives a great sense of communion. And once you stop sweating, wheezing, glowing red like a traffic light or all of the above, it will leave you feeling great for the rest of the day – physically, because you did it, and psychologically . . . because you did it.

Hackney Marshes parkrun is fast and flat but not without its challenges – out through the woods, where the road is longer than it looks because it follows a bend in the river, across the wide, open grassy space to the hairpin turn-back, which feels like the halfway point but is in fact probably only about two kilometres into your five, across and back through the woods, where – did I mention? – the road is longer than it looks because it follows a bend in the river – and then, just short of the finish, when you can guarantee every participant is, one way or another, pretty much spent – a harsh left turn, over the river, and out, then back, to tack on several hundred metres of necessary distance to make up for that early 'halfway' point.

Left turn and you're done. Easy.

I love it. It's addictive. And the more I do it, the more I find pleasure in the hardest moments – because that's where the real achieving happens. And – whisper it – that's the safe space where I can get a little bit competitive. It's at times like that when, over and above big beats and long playing times, the songs I listen to could do with a sprinkling of rage.

Perhaps 'rage' is too negative – but certainly a bit of *Raaargh!* energy. The 'tick follows tock' of Leftfield's 'Phat Planet'. The mad panic of the Prodigy's 'Voodoo People'. The primal guitar *tschplanng* of Nirvana's 'Smells Like Teen Spirit'.

The song that showed me which brief stretch of Hackney Marshes parkrun matters the most was 'We Are Rockstars' by Does it Offend You, Yeah? Whether you know the track or not, that title and the band's name give a very clear sense of the muscular insolence that's on offer here. It's Prodigy-esque; rock music played on electronic instruments, essentially. They pull together angry blasts of sound into one gleefully angry, funky whole: a dissonant bleep, like some kind of warning from a bit of heavy machinery; an overdriven riff that climbs up in just four beats from a bass note to a shriek; and a cowbell – who doesn't love a cowbell? – struck so hard it sounds like it should crack. What I'm saying is . . . *tuuune.*

As ever, this grey Saturday in Hackney's most spacious, countrified spot, I had set off fast, finding my pace, and my place in the pack, with a subconscious optimism that said, *This is a nice, steady, natural speed*, and then, not long after that, *Wow! I don't know how long I can keep this up*. But I kept it up all through the long woods and out across the north end of the Marshes, taking a momentary glance at the space-age, Olympic Park-dominated skyline to the south, with banging tunes all the way.

I don't know if people respond to the Marshes hairpin because they can see their fellow runners, because the illusion of a halfway point is unavoidable, or because it's just a good opportunity to reaffirm one's commitment to the distance and the pace, but some people come out of that turn *fast*. I used to think I must be slowing down, as people I had previously passed returned the favour, but, over several visits, I – with statistical justification – became more confident that I was holding steady, while they were accelerating.

So, this is where it always gets interesting. Who among these turn-of-speedy folk has the fuel in the tank to front out this push, and who will fade back to their earlier, natural spot once more? As 'We Are Rockstars' smashed into my ears that day, I saw this shakedown with more clarity than ever before. I was running as fast as I could – couldn't go faster, wouldn't go slower – so, no need to concern myself with that. All the speedsters held their pace back to the fringe of the woods – which, I suppose, must be around the real halfway point – and then I began to see it: *I'll be sliding past this one . . . I'll never catch that one* . . . It wasn't really competitiveness as much as observing how we would all end up fitting together. After all, in that moment at least, we were all running at very similar speeds.

I knew two things for sure: that the music was making this all very dramatic, and that it wasn't really anger I was hearing on my music-player, but joy. I had never noticed before how early the fate of the field was decided. Without thinking too hard about it, I guess I thought that we all cruised most of the way then sorted it all out in the final stages, but it's not like that at all; you sort it out in the middle, and in the final third you all just hang on as well as you can.

I reminded myself how the woods are longer than you'd think – well, not *you,* because I keep telling *you* how long that bit is, but . . . they're long – and hung on; turned left out to the second, merciless hairpin and hung on; turned left for the finish and, for the final 100 metres, hung on. A couple of people with admirable sprint-finishes nipped in ahead of me – of course – and we were done.

I've done Hackney Marshes parkrun ten, twenty times, and more than fifty parkruns overall, but that was the day I saw how and when the shakedown takes place, and now I see it often. It's different on different courses, but it's the same whichever week it is; the geography decides it, and whatever you've got in you on that day, that's when you find out about it.

A cowbell helps.

Another tune like this: The relentlessness of 'Crosseyed and Painless' by Talking Heads, with its metronomic, distorted guitar riff, comes to mind. But if you're actually cross-eyed and painless at the end of a parkrun, you're going too fast.

Another run like this: My favourite parkruns in other big cities of the UK are Cardiff, South Manchester and the one in Victoria Park, Glasgow. They're all intense.

19. EMBANKMENT MEMORIES
London 2018

I always feel guilty talking about the London Marathon.

To people who don't run marathons – runners and non-runners alike – it sounds like general showing off. To people who've tried to get a place in the ballot and been disappointed – and there are a lot of these – it's salt in the wound. Experienced distance athletes who've run marathons left right and centre like to make the point that 'There are other marathons!', and they often cross over with the next group, the large number of people in Britain who just disapprove of London in a non-specific way – disapproval that's exacerbated by the London-centric attitude of government and media. And by the price of booze here.

Even the organisers of the London Marathon are on my list of guilt triggers, because they wouldn't want it referred to as 'the London Marathon' – i.e. without naming the sponsor on the way. But I've done it – I've done it loads of times – and I love it. Run the Marathon, that is, not referred to it without the correct terminology. The *London* Marathon I mean. There are other marathons!

And I do love London. Its street-to-street changeability and its multiculturalism – in the broadest sense – appeal to my attention span, and it is beautiful, curvy and hilly with hardly any right-angled corners, full of history, great architecture, green spaces, water, trees.

It's also noisy, busy, dirty and expensive – I know, I know . . .

My own life story makes me particularly susceptible to London love. I spent my childhood here – but way out west, under the flight path for Heathrow. We were entitled to free double glazing because of the noise pollution – we didn't get it, but we were entitled to it; life was *loud*. So, I was a Londoner, but the city as we know it – not just 'the City', but the West End, all of it – glittered excitingly a dozen stops away up the Piccadilly Line. Then, when I was thirteen, we moved to the country. I was a teenager, and became a grown-up, elsewhere.

When I followed my girlfriend – now wife – back to town in the late nineties, I was twenty-five and I had literally forgotten I was a Londoner, in any emotional sense at least. I got to find myself as one all over again. I'm the perfect blend of native and incomer, all set to appreciate the capital's wonders. Plus, I'm terrible with money, so I rarely notice what I'm paying for my beer.

Thanks to Parkinson's UK, I've always been able to wangle a place in the Virgin Money London Marathon, and thanks to you lovely people I've always justified my presence there with a healthy injection of funds. I've done it eight times – despite the fact that the first time I fought it all the way, pacing it appallingly so that before I'd run ten miles I was ready to drop, hating the crowds – who hates the crowds? – and vowing I'd never do it again.

My dad was there that first time, with my mum at the twenty-five-mile mark. His Parkinson's meant it was the last time he could do the cheer-on-the-sidelines thing, and that day must have been pretty tough for him, but I'm so glad he got to see me doing what I now love so much, right there on the ground at that key spot. Of course, that day I just trudged angrily past – 'Yes, yes. Hello . . .' – taking my anti-marathon mood all the way round with me, and was more concerned with the heckler – 'Nice shorts!' – I passed at almost the same moment.

Now, I know that my mum and dad being there was a beautiful thing, as indeed was the heckle, and they've both stayed with me down the years. And I don't think it matters that I wasn't overly mindful of these wonders at the time; I'd just run twenty-five miles, so I think we can cut me a little slack.

Anyway, I broke my vow and did it again. Something

about the magnitude of the task of running a marathon means the hardship recedes in the memory – and surprises you all over again when you do another one. But something else makes you – or at least makes me – *still* want to do it all again. I went back two years later, ran a little better and was less grumpy. Now I was seeing a curve, the improvement of my running in the long game.

And then, in my pacy pomp, I went back *again* to try to run my fastest-ever marathon – remember this? I came pretty close, but my headphones died early on, which cost me dear, psychologically, and I very briefly walked, which I hugely regretted in retrospect. I'd run mile after mile in steady, speedy rhythm, but at the water station twenty-four-and-a-half miles in I took a bottle and walked while I drank it. The Parkinson's UK supporters' point was at twenty-five miles, so I was relying on my vanity to get me started again – no one of my acquaintance would see me not running – and, sure enough, I started again and didn't stop, clocking a final mile as fast as any I'd run – which is why, looking back at the stats, I despair for those thirst-quenching three minutes on the Embankment. That, and the fact that my cousins texted me a couple of hours later: 'We saw you walking at mile twenty-four. You looked like you were really suffering . . .'

That time was the fastest I've run the course, and will doubtless remain so, but I've run it again, and again, going well but weaker due to sundry injuries in between.

The last time I did it, in 2019, Paul Tonkinson and I recorded our podcast all the way round, which was really something; we caught an elusive experience there, to some extent at least. It's worth a listen, even as our conversation becomes more and more scattered and our primal sense of hanging-on-in-there more audible. You can hear the moment when we come up out of the underpass at Blackfriars Bridge – emerging to the blast of repetitive beats from the DJ booth there, the roar of the crowds and the first proper sight of the South Bank, the London Eye, Big Ben's tower. That's the crucible of the London Marathon, the beginning of the end, where, right in the heart of the place, amid the landmarks you see in old American TV shows and Hollywood movies, you start to realise that you're actually going to make it – with an awareness of what that's going to cost you, physically. On the podcast, going into that twenty-sixth mile, you can hear Paul encouraging the other runners with the simple, perfect mantra he'd stumbled upon: 'Push, push, push.'

A year before that, in 2018, it was hot – the hottest I've known it on Marathon day. *London* Marathon day – I do apologise. I'd done all the training, assiduously trying to get my strength back after the trials and tribulations of breaking a toe the summer before and struggling in the New York Marathon before Christmas as a result. But this hot weather was new – the sun came out blazing three days before the run and changed everything.

I'm nervous about running in hot weather – it can make things physically harder without one noticing, because this is hard stuff anyway; people can get hurt just by stubbornly – but reasonably – sticking to what they expect from themselves. I've seen it, in the Hackney Half Marathon one boiling June day a few years ago as the last miles snaked around the tree-free Olympic Park: godlike young athletes collapsing around me. That day, I learned: in the heat, slow down.

So that's how I approached the 2018 London Marathon. I put all concerns about my time to one side and held back a little. Still, by the time I got to twenty-ish miles or so, I had the fairly familiar feeling of not wanting to run another step. I'd run–walked from miles twenty-one to twenty-three in previous marathons, but on that hot day I felt a lot less guilty about it. It just seemed like good sense.

I started trying to run steadily again from mile twenty-three, but it was tough. I knew I needed something. It never fails to amaze me that the uplifting, trot-inducing power of a good song seems almost entirely undimmed by the efforts of running a marathon; the inspiration might only help for a short time, but there is always one tune that can give me the bump-start I need. As the sun blazed over London and I came out of Blackfriars Tunnel to see the Thames and the pods of the London Eye twinkling, the song 'Kick Jump Twist' by Sylvan Esso began to play, its minimalist bleeps and gently sung vocal immediately making me smile and creating a kind of ice-water-clear headspace where I could listen to the song while feeling a pin-sharp awareness of where I was and what was going on. It was like running in my own totally translucent bubble – and it felt good.

The lyrics struck a fine line between not really being lucid or directly relevant and throwing out ideas that chimed perfectly with the moment – shoes, pain, not caring but moving anyway, a lot like Paul's and my passionate, puffed-out, push-push-push nonsense a year later. And the song builds. Fast from the start, Sylvan Esso add beats in between the beats to push it up through the gears, and fill out the spindly web of sound with longer pulses of deeper synthesiser. Incredibly, I could feel myself begin to cruise. I was really running! If I could keep this up, I'd be at the finish line so, so soon.

The song sounds a bit sadder towards the end – but, of course, I love that, and it's still full and fast, like a spinning wheel. I felt joyful and strong and a little light-headed. A little way down from the twenty-five-mile mark, outside New Scotland Yard, my mum was at the barrier. I knew to look out for her but, in spite of that, I've missed family before – not just cousins, but my wife and children – and I think my clear bubble helped me spot her. I stepped over and stopped, confident I could start running again without seizing up – it was only for a moment, after all – and we hugged and had a little cry. This time I knew, in the moment, what mile twenty-five meant; the beginning of the end; the dawning knowledge that I was going to make it; the spot where dad had seen me and known all this too.

Parliament Square, Birdcage Walk, Buckingham Palace, the Mall – not far at all, but I can promise you, it seems further on the ground. The finish of the London Marathon – with apologies to those of you who don't want to hear it – is an incredible, incomparable thing. But my Marathon memories, particularly for runs receding into the past a bit now, always take me back to the twenty-five-mile mark.

(Sarcastic): 'Nice shorts!'

Another tune like this: It lacks the beats of 'Kick Jump Twist', so maybe wouldn't help as much so far into a marathon, but I absolutely love running to the crystalline heartbreak and scalpel-sharp production of Lykke Li's 'Hard Rain'.

Another run like this: The only marathon I've done which is anything like the London Marathon, with its community, social geography and filmic setting, is the New York Marathon – which is even harder to get a place in.

20. RUSH IN THE RAIN
York 2018

I can't believe I've got this far without mentioning Rush.

Do you know the work of this trio of Canadian virtuosi? Incredible musicians out of Toronto, playing initially Led Zeppelin-inflected, ever-more literary and grandiose widdly prog rock in the seventies, by the end of which they seldom created a piece of music that didn't last half an album, then finding muscular new purpose and clarity at the turn of the eighties with their reset album *Permanent Waves* and their masterwork *Moving Pictures*. For four decades they released regular albums, and shifted and changed their sound within their hugely talented, strictly three-man unit, creating music that was always good, often great and never, ever hip. The band's lyricist and drummer, Neil Peart, died in 2019, and for me it was one of those moments when a celebrity's death shows you how much they mean to you.

One of the first Rush songs I got into, years and years before I considered doing one, was 'Marathon' – probably the most literal song about running that I'll ever have on my playlist. And on the nose though it is, it's not just about running a marathon, but about a marathon as an allegory for life itself.

It's no cooler than it sounds, but it's great.

Rush's songs have featured heavily in my playlists ever since I started running, and like a lot of music that I enjoyed while growing up, I've forged a new and slightly different relationship with it now. My favourites have changed, and just hearing songs that I would once have listened to as part of an intense listen-through of a whole album on their own in a shuffled-up playlist changes their energy a lot.

I think the grace with which Rush aged, as humans and as a band, has been a roadmap for me, charting what, though it's been healthy, has clearly been some kind of midlife . . . let's not say 'crisis'; some kind of midlife . . . learning opportunity.

I've seen them perform live twice this century. The first time – on their thirtieth anniversary tour – I was really impressed by how objective they'd been about their own back catalogue, dismantling and putting it back together again with such a clear idea of what we, their audience, would enjoy. I didn't think of myself as a diehard fan, but they played song after song that made me think, *Yes! Of course they should play this one now!*

Maybe I was just in denial about how much of a fan I was.

Then, the next time I saw them, I had the opposite feeling – they still played an amazing, crowd-pleasing show, but it felt like they'd achieved it by doing exactly what *they* wanted to do. Yet at both shows they seemed completely in control of where they were, in life and on that night, taking their own long legacy and turning it into something fresh and entirely of the moment.

Good gigs.

In 2018 I ran the Yorkshire Marathon for the third time. Beyond the usual, enormous challenge of running all that way, this time was to be a test; after an injury in summer 2017, my two previous marathons – New York that winter and London in the spring of 2018 – had been difficult disappointments, and I had resolved that I would train harder than ever before for this event, and if I couldn't complete it in a way that was to my own satisfaction, i.e. running all the way, I would admit defeat – or at least admit my age – and retire from marathons for good.

That August, a couple of months before the run, I had an epiphany while I was training: if I was going to have any chance of success in this quest, doing enough was not going to be enough. I was completing all the anecdotally appropriate mileage and I felt my fitness was up to it – and that was the problem. My fitness had plateaued, and experience had shown that it was sitting at a level that could be described as not-quite-up-to-a-marathon.

I had to set my marathon training as the bar – my base level of fitness – and do more – further, faster. I had to push it. It wasn't a very welcome epiphany.

The marathon took place on the second Sunday in October, and it came round quickly. I strolled to my hotel on a limpid, almost summery Saturday evening and got an early night, getting off to sleep some time around eleven despite my nerves – only to be woken after half an hour by someone noisily settling into the room next door, watching something on TV that I gradually worked out was an old episode of *Who Wants To Be a Millionaire?* Ideal.

The next day started grey, with a light rain, but it soon changed – to an unrelenting deluge. I saw Tony Audenshaw – *Emmerdale* legend, top runner and all-round lovely man – before the start, and although he had a nasty, bronchial cough, he still insisted with infectious, grinning optimism that the weather was perfect for running; it wasn't windy, and the rain would keep us cool and even a little hydrated.

Sometimes I've got away with it, and other times it's got me into massive difficulties, but I always set off too fast in a marathon. I trot off the start line – where, due to my blagged celebrity place, I'm often lined up next to the foremost athletes in the event – and off we all go. The pace feels steady, normal, easy, and only much later do I realise I was going like the clappers, burning energy that might well have come in handy later on. By October 2018 I had done this enough times before to know it was an issue, but the Yorkshire Marathon starts downhill, which is a terrible temptation. Well, I felt like I was holding back. A bit.

And as soon as I started, I needed a wee – tiresome, but again, as you know, something of a habit, so I wasn't too bothered. I slipped off the course to the first Portaloos and I was in and out in moments, and now the temptation to nip was even stronger – I wanted to catch up with the people I'd been next to before! – but I held back as best I could. Getting on for five miles in, I spotted a pacer ahead of me, running steadily through the rain with his big flag flapping and a small coterie of runners around him. He was pacing them to finish in three hours and thirty minutes – fifteen minutes slower than my fastest time, on the same course four years before, but a bold aim, just within the realms of possibility, in autumn 2018. I had never run with a pacer, had no plan to and did not decide to do so now, but I did say to myself, *Do not pass the pacer. Stay behind him. But if you still want to go past him in, say, eighteen miles – go for it.*

The Yorkshire Marathon has about a fifth as many

runners as the big-city marathons I'd done; in those, the pacers are always surrounded by what can only be described as a massive cludge of runners – a cludge is like a phalanx, only stickier – and I'd always given them a wide berth. This pacer was trailed by a half dozen people or so, with plenty of room between them; maybe the rain helped. Anyway, it wasn't crowded, so I fell in behind.

I didn't meet any of these people, then or ever – I didn't even see their faces – but I got to really like them based on the backs of their heads, their running styles and my rain-and-distance-addled mind.

And now I was being paced; letting someone else think about how fast to go, on a course that, as you'd expect, showed me where to go – down lanes and dual carriageways I'd run before – in weather bound to make one retreat down into oneself, as if mentally huddled by the fire in a hut on a rock in the ocean. I couldn't have planned or chosen this psychological situation, but it was perfect for me. I ran on, unshackled from thought beyond the music in my ears, my beloved family of strangers-from-the-back, the road and the rain. Miles passed, one at a time, obviously, but with pleasing regularity. Then the halfway point ... Then sixteen miles ... Between eighteen and nineteen miles there is a turn back, up a hill you've just come down – the hardest stretch on the course – before you turn off onto a smaller road back to York, through the villages, at around twenty miles.

I was ready for it. I ran on. I missed the twenty-mile sign and was pleased but perturbed to see twenty-one. *I must be tired*, I thought, *but I mustn't stop or even slow down,* and in that moment I slipped into a momentary trance, or something like it; honestly, I looked around a moment – a minute? Some minutes? – later and suddenly I felt like I'd missed a bit, and I was refreshed. The mental me, huddled by the fire in the hut on the rock, had dozed off and had a nap while I ran on.

Despite this fresh feeling, I realised I was slowing slightly. My faceless phalanx family were slowly but surely drifting ahead, and there was very little I could do about it. I told myself that, when we were a little closer to the finish, I'd put on a turn of speed and catch them all up.

Yeah, right.

But I wasn't going to give myself a hard time. I had now run at three-hour-thirty-minute pace for twenty-two or twenty-three miles – so, not nothing – and I was still running. Slower and slower, it felt like, but still running.

Less than a mile from the finish of the Yorkshire Marathon you turn left at a traffic light and have to go up a massive hill. *Oof!* How very Yorkshire of them. And you, keen reader, are maybe thinking, 'This is where that Rush song about a marathon kicks in and brings him home' – but no, nothing as prosaic, I'm afraid. The Rush song that I always remember from that day had played much earlier, not long after the ten-mile mark, and it wasn't 'Marathon' but 'The Camera Eye' – which has nothing to do with running. But maybe it still gave me the clarity, the mindset, that I needed to run the race like I did.

'The Camera Eye' is the eleven-minute opener from side two of their aforementioned masterwork *Moving Pictures*. I really was in a good place to spend time with an elongated song about city rain that was both familiar from my youth and newly beloved; I'd even seen them play it live not so long before.

Such great music. Rush know how to rock – a sky-filling, distorted lead guitar, just slightly overdriven, propulsive bass and old-fashioned, must-have-taken-ages sequenced synthesisers, blibbing on the beat like something the Who might have done around the same time. But Rush don't rock like, say, Bon Jovi; there's no posturing, no one's going to be wearing leather or waggling their tongue around. This music is more serious than that, and less alpha-male. Neil Peart's loose and light yet immaculate drums underpin the whole, and despite their incredible technical prowess, the fact that there are just three of them, playing 'as live', means there's still room for lots of space in the sound they make. All manner of melodies, chords, slow bits and fast bits cruise by before singer-and-bassist Geddy Lee comes in with his totally distinctive, high, feminine voice and Peart's precision-tooled lyrics about New York and London – well, New York . . .

music, music, music . . . London – and the atmosphere the cities share.

It's a beautiful, obscure song, and I've long loved it, but that day in York, revelling in its riffs as I ran in the rain, I was particularly aware of how great it had been live. I saw Rush at the O2 in 2011, and during the show they played *Moving Pictures* in its entirety. They smashed out this rich, warm perfect album from three decades earlier, playing it as tightly as can be – of course – but with joy and verve. They were clearly loving it. It got me thinking how, despite the apparently backwards-looking, nostalgic nature of the show, playing the songs that well, at that moment, they were as fresh as anything.

When you're older and more experienced, maybe it takes a little more focus and skill to fully access your strength and you might have to take more care to be present in the here and now than you would have as a youngster – but, if you can do these things, you'll be at least as powerful as you've ever been . . . I thought to myself.

And I ran on.

What got me up that final hill, still running, was not music but vanity; someone recognised me and called encouragement from the sidelines, and, without thinking, I unzipped my little rain jacket, took off my silly cap and fluffed up my sodden quiff as best I could – I needed to look sharp for the finish-line cameras. Then, just like that, I was done.

A few metres beyond the finish line I saw my pacer, so I got a chance to thank him, which was nice, despite the fact that he, of course, had no idea I'd been toddling along behind him all that way.

I finished five seconds under three hours and thirty-three minutes. I'd run faster marathons, but I'd never run one better.

I passed the test.

I ran on.

Another tune like this: I listen to loads of Rush when I run. 'Tom Sawyer', 'Digital Man', 'Xanadu' and 'Between the Wheels' are all particular favourites.

Another run like this: The Yorkshire Marathon – the first time I did it, in 2014, described earlier, the time after this, in 2019, which I'll tell you about shortly, or the other time I did it – the time when Paul Tonkinson went to the toilet without stopping at a toilet. I was certainly glad to be a few minutes behind him that day.

21. A VERY HEAVEN

Auliston Point 2019

I'm very lucky to have old friends – I mean longstanding friends, not elderly friends, although they are actually on the old side – who own a cottage on the Morvern Peninsula, on the west coast of Scotland. The Old School House looks out across the Sound of Mull to Tobermory, where you can see the pretty-coloured houses by day and the twinkling lights at night. It's absolutely heavenly, and from time to time we get to stay there. When we do, the epic journey alone makes it feel like visiting another, more magical world. It's a full two-day drive from London, and once you're beyond the cities of Scotland, first the scenery swells into lochs, mountains and moors that mock even the Cumbrian countryside you drove past yesterday, then the road lengthens and fades; a busy tourist road reaches a ferry, then drops to one lane with passing places on the other side, although suddenly, thankfully, cars coming the opposite way become rare. Meanwhile, the distance between villages – there aren't any towns on the mainland this far west – stretches to ten, twelve, twenty miles. Chances are you will actually see a stag or a golden eagle. By the time you reach your destination, it could be Narnia.

It's the best place in the world to run. Even the daunting scale is actually an advantage; not far beyond the cottage, the road becomes a gated track following the coast first north-west, then directly east. 'I'll just pop to the point and back' is fifteen, sixteen miles – such beautiful, changeable miles that they fly by, even with my greedy attention span. Meanwhile, an incline that swells to a hill bigger than anything in London, Birmingham or Glasgow creeps slowly up under your feet almost without you noticing.

One pristine August morning in 2019, I set off on this route. I had done it before, so I knew the way and how wonderful it was, but this weather was better – perfect, in fact. My wife was also keen to run, but she was working, so we arranged for her to run out after me – I would turn back, meet her along the way, and we'd come back together.

The cottage is just above a little bay; you can hear the waves lapping at the shore. Carrying on along the lane you arrived down, first you reach a stone bridge where the river tumbles, peaty-brown breaking white over the rocks, to the sea. The tarmac ends but the road is still gravelled; there are other buildings scattered around here – beautiful houses, plus a small church on a rocky outcrop where, as well as services, cool folky concerts take place. And there's a whisky distillery. I'm telling you, it's idyllic.

You fork gently right, keeping all these places between you and the sea, and cruise past them at the bottom of the heathery hillside. Here the trick of scale is in play. In my memory, this part of the run is a trot up a pretty driveway – and that's true, it is – but it goes on for at least two miles, steadily climbing all the way.

Beyond the green roofs of the distillery, an exciting change: a gate, which lets you out on to open moorland. It's a deer-proof gate – not heavy, just narrow wood and barbed wire, but tall, with a person-sized side gate set at an angle that means gravity will keep it shut. You don't see these in Hackney. And chances are you will see deer once you're through – slim and graceful, shy of course, but not as desperately elusive as the ninja deer that vanish into the woodland of, say, the Chilterns. They'll clock you with a sharp look and an attentive ear pricked up to the sky, stay stock-still for thirty seconds . . . then cruise gently on up the hillside, trusting their camouflage.

The gravel's stopped now. The track continues as a rutted, muddy lane, but it's still solid; cars and trucks go this way sometimes, even trailers with yachts on. Life goes on beyond proper roads up here. For running, it's fantastic: you're deep in wild country, with a good solid, cruisable surface underfoot. You're now hundreds of feet above the sea, and instead of hearing waves lapping, you're looking at a solid expanse of blue on your left. As you leave the few houses behind and run on, the Sound of Mull spreads out, Loch Sunart joins it from your right, and miles of ocean open up between the Isle of Mull and the Ardnamurchan peninsula, drawing the eye directly west to the Atlantic.

On this scintillating August day, I saw first that there was much more to the town of Tobermory than could be seen from our windows at the cottage I'd left behind. I could see the whole, lovely place spreading down the hillside to a sparkling bay full of bobbing boats, across the Sound, which, from up here, showed its full width. A car ferry chugged up the middle between me and the distant town, overtaking me gradually and changing its bearing from north-west to full west, heading right down the middle, directly away from me, straight out to sea. So much brilliant blue – the sea and the sky in that intense sunshine; so much pure, beautiful space, and all beyond my verdant, picture-book pathway and the long grass, rocky outcrops, bracken and the occasional hardy tree dropping below me to the shore. It was almost a relief to turn my back on this breathtaking scene and head east.

It was still gorgeous. The track drops to cross a stream, then climbs more noticeably, zigzagging to cross the shoulder of the long ridge of hills it has been so gradually ascending. Here the track is neatly engineered, cut into the heathery hillside, with a pine forest covering the slope downhill between you and the sea to the north.

The climb becomes gentler as the lane bounces along the northern edge of Morvern, following the contour as it rolls in and out of the main body of the hill, streams dropping under the track and through a series of gorges and gullies to the sea. At this point you feel like you're just getting started, and the urge to follow the path all the way to the end is strong, but on this run it was time to turn back. As I reached the near-imperceptible highest point, I took a moment, did a heathery wee, and headed back the way I had come.

I am not religious. I am not even really as spiritual as these stories might have you think – but, my goodness, if this was a journey further and further into Narnia, then this was the point where Aslan, or a lamb – let's face it, C. S. Lewis, some animal who's actually Jesus – would turn up and say, 'Yeah, I think you get it now.' Turning back down that hill, literally and figuratively, I could see the curvature of the earth. As a herd of deer loped into the woods on my right, 'Low Burn' by Underworld began to play.

'Low Burn' is later Underworld, not a nostalgic tune to take me back to my dancing days, but one I've discovered through running. It begins with long, filmic notes, building only gently to a repetitive, dancey groove – not so you'd notice – with cinematic strings and woodwind notes gliding across the top as Karl Hyde intones positive, mantra-like messages. Repeating them like this, low in the mix, sounding just a tiny bit sinister, upbeat though they are, keeps these lyrics from being twee; discourages resistance; lets them in. After all, if they were written on a cushion, for example, you know I'd reject them.

I ran down the steepening hill like a rocket, but a rocket powered by some quiet, cool fuel; like a hybrid car – a rocket Toyota Prius. At a physical level, I was entirely pumped. I had run a long, steady warm-up, on a gradual incline, then pushed up a hard, aerobic climb; even as I flew down this track, someone in a gym somewhere had set their treadmill to provide this same, immaculate workout. At an experiential level, I was running straight towards – into – this enormous, stunning sea-and-land-and-skyscape. Even the fact that I'd spent a while looking at it already on the way up enhanced this high, because I could take it all in at a glance, already imprinted on my soul as it was, while keeping an eye on where to put my pounding feet next.

At an emotional level I felt . . . understanding. I knew that my body was throbbing with blood and adrenaline, that I was looking at a scene as beautiful as any I would see at any time, and that I would remember this. I knew that I am a runner who needs music to transcend the mechanics of the task, and that this music had the optimum blend of drama, joy, wistfulness and rhythm. I had been running long enough – on this day, and in life – to *get* that this ambient dance music forged a spiritual and physical link between me in my forties and me in my twenties, and in both cases I was accessing joy. No, more than that: love.

I was loved up.

Still running like the wind, I had a tiny cry, sweat and tears mingling on my temples. On top of all this incredible awareness, in this memorable moment, I had remembered that back at the deer gate I would meet my wonderful wife, and she, the love of my life, would understand – completely understand – this elation. What a hug I would give her, sweaty or not! Taking a last look between the headlands to the Atlantic, I sped to the gate, back to reality. Holiday reality, at least.

She wasn't there; she was at an entirely different gate. I hadn't explained myself very well; there is another gorgeous route, another deer gate out onto the hillside, and she was waiting there. Ah well. I was much too high to be disappointed. It was funny! My quasi-religious moment gently skewered, I ran on back to her, as she ran back down to me, still in the sunshine, still listening to great music, still cruising downhill. There's always another loving hug to be had, another beautiful view, another pumping tune at the perfect moment. Run on.

Another tune like this: Ambience, dance music grooves and an upbeat but subtly produced lyric can also be found on Fluke's 'Groovy Feeling (Make Mine a 99)', which I once listened to at the top of a mountain as the sun rose over the sea below me. Another great, twenty-first century Underworld tune to run to is 'Jumbo', with its sample of guys talking about Walmart having a sale on vests, of all things.

Another run like this: I once ran up the long hill out of Brighton to the racecourse, then along the South Downs way over the tops, with views of Lewes to the north, before turning right and winding down towards the glittering sea, eventually reaching it at Saltdean, after being serenaded by a skylark in a cloudless sky. That was pretty special.

22. WHAT DO YOU GET WHEN YOU CROSS A HALF MARATHON WITH A GRAND PRIX?

Oulton Park 2019

During the 2018 London Marathon – specifically, during the long, hard miles between Poplar and the Tower, when you've run twenty miles and turned towards the finish but you've still got ridiculously, unimaginably far to go – I made a decision.

At the moment I made it, I was walking – well, dividing my time between running very slowly and walking – for just a couple of miles. I didn't feel too bad about this – as far as I was concerned, all bets were off because of how hot it was out there – but it was a lot like the rather more tortured walking I'd done around the same time the marathon before that, in New York in November 2017. And I set great stock in running for the whole length of a marathon. I hadn't often done it, but I had done it, and there in London's hot home straight I was concerned that I couldn't do it any more.

So my decision was this: once I'd reached that finish line, I would sign up for one more marathon, the Yorkshire Marathon that autumn, and go all out for a fit, fast one, running all the way round, and if I found myself having to walk some of it, that would be it for me: no more marathons. I would retire from the distance, happy with the ones I'd done, and let it go.

It was a key moment in my running life. This apparent resignation would ultimately lead to a whole new phase for me – and, among other moments and adventures, it led me to Oulton Park in Cheshire. The best part of a year after my resolution – and, tellingly, a few months on from the Yorkshire Marathon – I had booked myself into a half marathon as part of my training for the 2019 London Marathon; 'Just when I thought I was out, they pull me back in'.

My run that day was part of an events company called RunThrough's 'Running Grand Prix': different distances – 5k, 10k, half marathon, marathon – all run at the same time on a motor-racing circuit. Not at the same time as the cars, though – that sounds like a particularly dangerous episode of *Top Gear*.

Now, usually I'm not someone who enjoys repetition in a run, but this would be all about the laps. I was ready;

they would be long, interesting laps, and that was just one of the things that would make this event something a bit different for me.

On the Saturday afternoon of a weekend doing shows at the Manchester Comedy Store, I picked up a teeny-tiny hire car, and on the Sunday morning I tootled out into the classy countryside of Cheshire. As I parked up at the circuit, it began to rain – not too much at first, but as the morning went on it got pretty heavy. It wasn't too bad, mind. It was a lovely, mild spring rain, and between my memory of the heat of London and virtually swimming round that autumn marathon in an authentic Yorkshire deluge, I reckoned I could handle it.

It was a really nice, friendly event, too. Despite the fact that we weren't anywhere public, the organisers had made sure there were cheery supporters dotted round the course, smiling and jingling bells and tambourines, and even a band playing under a gazebo. What's more, the runners themselves were a diverse lot drawn from the whole community, from Couch-to-5k-ers completing their challenge to club runners going for near-Olympic PBs, via everyone in between.

My race would be five laps of the track, each lap being a little over two-and-a-half miles – 2.692, actually, which, multiplied by five, comes to 13.46, so they must have adjusted the start and finish lines to reduce the distance by 0.36 and hit the requisite 13.1 ... Still with me, maths fans?

Someone, of course, really had leaned into the arithmetic necessary to not only give each runner the right race length, but also to dot out signs along the course telling us exactly how far we'd come and had yet to go. It was brilliantly bewildering; I was running past apparently arbitrary signs – 3 kilometres to go! 9 miles! 1 mile! 8 kilometres! 36 feet! 4 fathoms! – and I felt like the genius mathematician in a Hollywood film, numbers and symbols flying around their head as they tap their chin with a pencil and sparkly, computer-esque music plays. Except I had no idea what these numbers meant.

It was really good for me; the end result was that I got exactly the information I needed, but only by forgetting about it. Obsessing unnecessarily was impossible – there was too much contradictory input – but when I knew roughly where I was anyway, signs that were relevant to me would make sense, and I'd see that the others ... were for the others. Or maybe I did the wrong number of laps. We'll never know for sure, but though I may not be Rain Man, Little Man Tate or the *Beautiful Mind* guy, I can, I like to believe, slowly count to five.

The other runners also gave me a really healthily confusing perspective; within a mile of the start I'd lost track of who had started with me, so I never really knew who was running the same distance. Sometimes I'd tune into someone running at a similar pace, but I had no idea where they were in their story.

The track was great. It swooped down in a series of long curves past patches of woodland and a lake dotted with interesting waterfowl, then banked round a hairpin bend before coming straight back, this time going up and down rather than side to side, with a couple of challenging inclines that were over too quickly to really feel like hills – although they must really flip your stomach when you go fast over them in a car. There was far too much going on for it to feel relentless once we started going round again, and the laps were long enough that finishing one felt like I was getting somewhere.

The reliable and unchanging tarmac underfoot suited my steady spirit, too. I found I could maintain my speed up those inclines just by gritting my teeth and hanging on for the luxury of getting over the top and down the other side. And once I'd done that on the first lap, I had to do it every lap, naturally.

My running brother, Paul Tonkinson, had offhandedly said in a text that I should try to speed up a bit in the second half, which was great advice, and probably not something I would have asked of myself, so I was resolved to change up a gear going into the fourth lap. I hadn't been particularly dawdling, so it was quite a big ask, but as I passed the stand and the pit lane – or whatever they call it – I put my head up, lifted my arms a little higher and pushed the pace. The dropping, curving swoop, and my lack of physical imagination, meant once I'd set that pace, I kept it.

As I came around the hairpin on that fourth lap, having done around ten miles, but in an unusually luxurious state of not really knowing that, I was feeling a bit spacey – from a combination of the distance I'd done and the pace I was making. I was still happy, but I needed a boost going into the bumps. The great thing about listening to music when you're really digging in like that is that you're emotionally vulnerable, so the right song will hit you like a drug. As I climbed, Sigrid's 'Strangers' started to play. The young Norwegian singer-songwriter's music is right up my alley anyway – lyrics open-hearted but clear-eyed, vocals and beautifully produced music more powerful than ethereal. Add to that the wonderful memories I had of taking my brilliant, then twelve-year-old daughter to see her at Brixton Academy a few weeks before, and we were onto a winner. I listened carefully to the song, not knowing it all that well yet. The beginning sounds like a rain cloud, and Sigrid immediately talks about the clichéd romance of rain in films. It caught and seemed to mock my would-be wistful moment perfectly. Then, as I came over the brow of the hill, the juddering chug of the sequenced bassline kicked in, held back till half way through the chorus in a great bit of in-song delayed gratification. *Bwaauuugh!* With that blast of power, I was sorted for the rest of the lap, despite there being another mile of it.

So, now I was into the fifth and final loop . . . probably. It might have been the penultimate lap, or an extra one, but let's assume not. I felt good. I was still enjoying myself, and there was less and less time for that to change. The rainy, black tarmac of the course felt like a friend, and rather than growing weary of it, I cherished the chance to take my leave of the trees, the lake, the banked-up hairpin bend and the sodden guy with the tambourine whose cheeriness was beginning to slip, as I passed them all one last time. I had fallen in with some other runners going at about the same speed as me; there was a guy a little ahead of me who, I'd worked out, was also doing the half, and I liked his pace and style, so I resolved to do my best to follow him in.

As I went over the bumps for the last time, a real banger played – 'Two Months Off' by Underworld. I love it. It's propulsive and it's long, so I knew it would really help me along. But I thought fondly back a lap to the Sigrid track. Without planning to, I started singing 'Strangers' in my head along with the 'Two Months Off' in my ears. What a mash-up! One of the best I've heard – except I haven't; to this day it has only ever played in my head, but that feels appropriate in the context of my memories of this dreamlike day.

I saw the '1 mile to go' sign and I knew it meant me. I

locked on to my steady friend and waited for the side lane to the finish line. I'd already seen it; I'd run past it four times . . . and there it was. I went in – but he did not. 'Mate,' I nearly called out, 'you're missing it!', but he must have been doing a marathon or twenty miles, or having a senior moment – I don't know.

I crossed the line and got my medal. What a fun thing it was, nothing like any other half marathon I've done. Grounded in good music, steady tarmac, strong running, but still pretty blooming surreal. It turned out I'd damaged my timing chip, so I never got an official finish time, but I don't mind – that feels right. And as well as my mildly crazy memories, I've got that medal.

I think I've got that medal.

Where is that medal?

Another tune like this: This will offend someone, some-where, but I love Sigrid's take on 'Everybody Knows', the Leonard Cohen song, which she recorded for the execrable film *Justice League*. It's not really like her other singles, which are also great for running; it's a slow, doom-laden piano plod – but it's a cracking song and she sings the hell out of it.

Another run like this: Five times round a Grand Prix course? I know of no other run like this! Let me know if you do.

23. COACH GEORGE

Yorkshire 2019

You'll have noticed that I've done the Yorkshire Marathon several times. I don't know quite how this happened, but I'm into it. York, where it starts and finishes, is a wonderful city, but I have no particular connection with it – no family in the area; I didn't study there. I can't remember now whether I approached Parkinson's UK about getting me a place, the first time I did it, or they approached me, but, either way, since then it's become a bit of a fixture in my running calendar – the northern England autumn counterpoint to the London Marathon in the spring.

I am well aware of how lucky I am to be able to get marathon places through both my job and a friendly charity – the London Marathon in particular. There are runners knocked back in the ballot year after year who, on hearing me breezily talking about doing it 'again' or 'every year', get a tic in one eye and begin to giggle like Inspector Dreyfus in the *Pink Panther* films. Apologies.

But that relationship is defining for me. If it wasn't for Dad, and Parkinson's UK, I might never have run more than ten miles. Why would I? I don't know if you've experienced a marathon, but as a veteran, let me give you a bit of insider knowledge: a marathon is really far. But that guilt-trip I laid on myself a decade ago has led me to over a dozen of them and, beyond that, defined all my multifarious physical exercise, my day-to-day existence and my overall outlook on life.

In October 2019 I lined up for the start of the York-shire Marathon for the fourth time. Actually, I didn't line up, because five minutes before it began, my old friend from the event, Tony 'Bob off *Emmerdale*' Audenshaw and I were whisked off to do a short interview and *start the race*! Seriously, we had no idea this was about to happen. Looking back, this seems amazingly relaxed of the organisers; someone more famous must have failed to turn up. But if you watch the video of the 2019 event on YouTube, look out for the flag being waved over the start line – it's me doing the waving. Then you glimpse me running past – they opened a gap in the fence, I slipped through and got going.

What a great way to begin a big distance event! The start line of a long run is a place where, normally, one has to deal with the psychology of being a huge bundle of nerves, training, planning, plasters and Vaseline – simultaneously knowing that by the time any of that stuff matters, a couple of hours and many, many miles will have passed and you'll be somewhere else entirely, mentally and physically. Instead of this strange, slightly difficult moment, I had five minutes of fun with a friend and a flag foisted on me.

I'm sure that contributed to my cheery, easy mindset for the run, a mindset that lasted . . . well, until I'd run really far. Plus, it's a lovely event, full of great people, in a gorgeous part of the world – and the weather was nice.

As usual, we made our way through York and out east through some pretty villages. Before too long a runner trotted up alongside me and said, 'I've got a cheque for you for Parkinson's UK – I'll give it to you later', which he did. A stranger, carrying a contribution for me – what a beautiful thing. What a sweaty cheque.

Oh, and after three failed attempts in the previous years, I got a high five from the village vicar who doles them out religiously ever year. Hashtag: blessed.

The route of the Yorkshire Marathon meanders eastwards through the countryside for just over half its distance before hooking back on a big, straight road towards – and nearly past – York for six miles, doubling back a second time and returning to villages and lanes for the final, tough few miles, where the gradual build-up of the city really helps bring you home.

Until you turn left up that dastardly hill right at the end.

I'd set off at a good pace – i.e. probably too fast – but I'd held it, and after the first ten miles I was still going well, appreciating my knowledge of the course, reconciling myself to the fact that there were a couple more miles of winding through the woods before the halfway point. But I was beginning to feel it: I was in the midst of the marathon runner's shift from a common-or-garden good, hard run to an uncommon feat of endurance. That's when I heard the song I'm remembering now. I don't think it had been on my running playlist for long; it's not an obvious, aerobics-class house tune, nor does it bring the high drama I look for in the film music or rock songs I have on there. I had put it on the list for two reasons: firstly to take myself by surprise and secondly to remember the late, great George Michael.

I love George Michael and his music. He is the beloved singer-songwriter in my life that the teenage me would have expected Morrissey to turn out to be, if you see what I mean. There was nothing cool, let alone alternative about Wham! to appeal to me; the Smiths were where I lived back then. But as you get older, you learn that fashion is just fashion – quality abides. And that Morrissey is a horrible bigot.

The track that arrived in my ears as the marathon began to bite was 'Freedom! '90', one of the singles from gorgeous George's first solo album, *Listen Without Prejudice*

Vol. 1. I'd always known it was a great song, but I probably only started occasionally deliberately listening to it after he sang it . . . on top of a taxi? No, that was the Spice Girls . . . at the closing ceremony of the 2012 London Olympics. I'd never listened properly to the lyrics until 2019. They're great. It's a statement of intent, celebrating the success of Wham! but making it clear that, from here on in, he's going to be himself, take it or leave it – a neat summary of where he was at creatively that also, consciously or unconsciously, works as a take on being a gay man who's a sex symbol to an entire generation of teenage girls. This was several years before he was entrapped and outed – and took fantastic ownership over the whole sordid business – in 1998.

This is the kind of stuff I think about when I'm running.

In the leafy lanes of Yorkshire, I heard George Michael sing the middle eight of 'Freedom! '90', a minor-key moment where he considers the deal with the devil he made to make it big with Wham! – how the road to heaven felt like the road to hell. 'Nice,' I thought. 'That's me, here, right now.'

By the time I'd tuned into the words he'd written and sung thirty years before, George Michael had been gone for nearly three years – he died on Christmas Day 2016. Even before then, fitness-wise, he wasn't really a runner's role model. I chuckled internally, thinking how twisted it was of me to invoke him as my mental coach, and I characterised him as part of a squad – along with Mama Cass from the Mamas & the Papas, Jimi Hendrix and Amy Winehouse – singing me on. I realised that this was all probably a way – a very silly way – of relating to the memory of my dad, who had died only about six weeks before this run. Now I saw myself as Father Ted in the scene where, beset by troubles, he runs along the beach as the spirits of Mrs Doyle, Father Jack and an angry fisherman float and quote around him, and Father Dougal floats up, can't think of anything to say, and floats away again.

I laughed out loud as the huge, gospel-infused chorus swelled again, and carried on running my best, happiest marathon in years.

Another tune like this: 'Outside', the hit single George Michael used to take ownership over the whole gossipy debacle of his being outed, is a great song with an effortless groove. That's just one example; he was a superb songwriter – the whole of *For The Feet*, the second CD in his *Ladies & Gentlemen* greatest hits compilation, is very running-playlist-friendly.

24. CATCHING UP

Southsea 2019

As the nineties began, so did the band Orbital, knocking out fantastic singles initially recorded under the stairs in their family home and staying at the vanguard of dance music as it crept into the mainstream, not least because of their televised headline set at Glastonbury '94. But I didn't like them much at the time. I can't for the life of me think why now; they were, and still are, right up my alley. Joyous yet sophisticated dance music with witty samples and uplifting tunes? Yes please!

I think, back in the day, they so embodied the credo of rave culture that their very existence made me feel like I was missing out. They are, after all, named after the M25. I liked the idea of all that but, out in the Oxfordshire countryside where I lived at that time, it was all a bit once-removed for me. My friends and I liked the idea of all that partying – everyone I knew fancied themselves as a DJ – and we often spent nights out in the fields . . . but it was just us, and they were just fields.

And all that Second Summer of Love house and post-house dance music was *very* new to us, in a way that's hard to remember now. My social group needed the musical gateway drug that was the baggy, Manchester scene; having grown up listening to the Smiths and all manner of indie, non-rock guitar music, the Stone Roses and Happy Mondays made much more sense to our ears than the repetitive beats being served up just a little bit closer to London.

Out there in the country, we still had plenty of time for the original hippie sound; I was as likely to hear Pink Floyd or Hawkwind or even Gong as I was to hear the Chemical Brothers, the Prodigy or Orbital. And those psychedelic rock bands are nothing if not serious. My first love was the Cure, and, as the eighties drew to an end, I knew their records better than I knew myself. I still love a lot of their songs, but 'joyous, yet sophisticated dance music with witty samples and uplifting tunes' they are not.

Meanwhile, Orbital, along with sounding – heaven for-fend – happy, were chewing up pop culture and spitting it out again in new and exciting forms, with the kind of post-modern self-awareness that would, once the internet hit, ultimately come to define *all* of popular culture, from

Hollywood blockbusters to Netflix series to all kinds of music, from Taylor Swift to Tame Impala. Back then, Orbital would take fantastic, not particularly cool songs from our youth – Bon Jovi's 'You Give Love a Bad Name', Belinda Carlisle's 'Heaven Is a Place on Earth' – and reconfigure them into huge, anthemic dance crescendi.

Why did I not *love* this?!

Well, I wasn't there – and I wasn't ready. They say 'What's for you won't go past you', and, sure enough, I got into Orbital in the end. Now I have the luxury of listening to them as part of my life in the twenty-first century, without having to trawl through any associated bad memories of my own foolishness as a youngster. What's more, after breaking up for a little while, they've come back together and steadily produced new music – and done live shows – in the last couple of years.

In 2018 they dropped – see? See how twenty-first century I am? – 'P.H.U.K.U.', and it's one of my favourite tunes to run to. I love that this music is not only a newer release from them, but that it post-dates my own realisation that I would get more pleasure running while listening to dance music than I ever did dancing to it back in the day.

And it sounds ... right. The music is compelling, uplifting, but the vocal sample is angry, political; rabble-rousing, essentially, speaking to Orbital's countercultural credentials – they protested the Poll Tax on *Top of the Pops* – but in a way that gets the party started just as effectively as the beats and the buzz-saw synths. I love the way that, melodically, its echoes go right back to their breakthrough tune 'Chime', but that rather than making you think of some long-lost, did-it-ever-really-happen rave from a quarter of a century ago, these guys are smashing it live with this stuff right now, up to and including the 2020 lockdown, during which they played at a 'stay at home rave' hosted by United We Stream and the Haçienda for Manchester-based victims of the pandemic.

I've listened to the tune a lot myself in recent weeks, during said lockdown, on my appropriately-socially-distanced runs. I think it's because, even when I'm literally avoiding everyone in the world, I can't help but feel I'm part of something when I hear it. And that's also why it caught and enhanced a moment I felt at Southsea parkrun last year.

Southsea parkrun sits beautifully in the middle of a snapshot of my life as lived in 2019. I had performed at the nearby Wedgewood Rooms on Friday night – a glorious, always slightly rowdy gig in a music venue that I love to play, would-be rock star that I am. It's like coming home, but with new people every time, and always feels fresh and fun despite the fact that I first played it twenty years ago. I didn't find it as glorious back then – I had to grow up into it; that might be part of why I still love it now, I suppose.

Not having a car to drive straight home in any more, and loving a parkrun, after the show I stayed over at a hotel right by South Parade Pier, the heart of Southsea's classic south-coast seafront, and located near the beginning – and end – of the local Saturday morning 5k.

I got up really early, without a hangover, not having drunk on the Friday night – a once-inconceivable manoeuvre – so as to get myself together enough for the nine o'clock parkrun start not to feel too much like a short, sharp kick to the soul. I went down to the breakfast buffet and drank coffee as the sun rose over the sea, but I didn't eat anything – another once-inconceivable manoeuvre, but quintessential weekend behaviour for me by 2019.

Southsea parkrun is a simple there-and-back along the promenade – two-and-a-half kilometres to the lovely volunteer who's gone down there just to smile and wave us all through – 'Thank you, marshal' – and two-and-a-half kilometres back. There's nowhere to hide from the distance, or from the difficulty of maintaining any pace in the second half that you might have had in the first, but everyone in the run, from the fastest to the slowest, gets to spend a moment face-to-face with a selection of their running brothers and sisters as we all pass in opposite directions. I'm sure the very fastest runners are barely aware of this – and good luck to them in their exertions – but I love it. Not that I'm not one for running the distance as fast as I can – but the faces I see after a turn-back in any event are always heartening to me, and a useful distraction from the run as the distance bites.

That sunny, windy day in Southsea – the wind was behind us on the way out and there to hinder us on the way back – Orbital's 'P.H.U.K.U.' soundtracked the last kilometre or two, and it was wonderful. Having accepted the challenge of the wind, I was hanging on in there, heading back towards that pier, trying to maintain my pace; I had just overtaken a guy, so now I had to assume he was just behind me, ready to judge me if I didn't keep it up. It was great music to hear at that moment, keeping me happy even as my body began to seriously complain about what I was asking of it. Looking back, I think I was going steady, but this stranger had the stronger finish and with a couple of hundred metres to go, when I'd stopped thinking about him, he came back past me – and it was all I could do to stay anywhere near him.

As he went over the finish line, someone else with more in the reserve than me also slipped past, so I wasn't even the next in after the guy who had so fleetingly been my chief competitor. Did either of those people have any awareness of me, or the other person, or was it just them and the finish line? No matter; for a moment I felt us all there together and, emboldened by the anthem in my ears, I would happily have given them both a hug. But I didn't. Hey, we were all sweating, we were all strangers and this was not a field somewhere just outside London circa 1994. It was back over the road to the hotel for me, to stretch, shower and check out, before catching a train to my next gig.

But I remembered that moment, hearing 'P.H.U.K.U.' while I was out running in these strange, Glastonbury-, marathon- and parkrun-free times, and I appreciated the song taking me back there and beyond.

In 2013, one week before I ran the London Marathon for a second time, the terrorist bombing at the marathon in Boston happened. It was awful – such pointless, misanthropic violence at this particular place, this moment of communal joy and achievement. From my peripheral perspective, it felt like the London event had been tainted, maybe spoiled. But once we all started running together, I realised two things: firstly, that running helps us process darkness and despair and to alchemise them into joy; we see this whenever someone runs further than they ever have in their life in memory of someone they have lost, but it's also true day to day, in the mental health benefits of not much fancying a run but going anyway, and being glad you did. Secondly, I realised that day that every one of the forty thousand-ish runners in the London Marathon had their own deeply personal, sometimes totally tragic, story. There were people running in London who had run in Boston the week before, and others who were so deeply embroiled in their own dramatic lives that they might have been barely aware of the bombing. Nevertheless, none of that changed the fact that we were all out there together, en masse, doing this one difficult but simple thing.

And that's always true, isn't it? We are individuals, but together we make up this one great mass of humanity, doing this one difficult but simple thing: living. Nineties rave, big-city marathon, your local parkrun, locked down or out and about, we are all brothers and sisters and we are all strangers.

All here doing this alone, all in it together.

Another tune like this: Get hold of a live version of Orbital's 'Halcyon', with Belinda Carlisle and Bon Jovi. Listening to the sound of the best party in the world, while you're running as fast as you can, is a beautiful thing.

Another run like this: There's another wonderful communal but deeply unforgiving seafront parkrun in Brighton and Hove, on the promenade at Hove Lawns. There and back, past and back, there and back, past and back. Nowhere to hide.

25. NORTH THROUGH BORTH

Aberystwyth 2020

In January 2020, I hired a car and cruised into Wales, then out across the North of England, for a run of gigs – twice. The second of these trips, at the end of the month, took me to Aberystwyth, a town I have always liked a lot. It's so offhandedly dramatic – at the end of a long, long road, or railway line, its pretty, curving bay located between the rocky headland to the north and the castle to the south, and, over the horizon, ninety miles west: Ireland. If this arrangement wasn't quite so far into Wales, there'd be more fuss about it.

As it is, it's a laid-back town with a big university where I've always imagined it would be great to be a student – a geographically ready-made bubble to go and live in for a couple of years while you work out what you like doing with your time. Towns that aren't on the way to anywhere always have a character all their own.

When I first started touring as a comedian, I played the student circuit, and Aberystwyth – along with Hull, also at the end of the road to the sea – was widely renowned as the loveliest of student gigs. And this was before widespread internet use, let alone Netflix, so the comedy was well attended – what else were those guys going to do with their time? It was a joy to make that long journey and be rewarded with those big laughs at the end of it.

These days I don't do so many student gigs, as they tend to make me feel about a thousand years old. Instead, in Aberystwyth I play the Arts Centre – a glorious round space with an audience of people up to and including my own age – on the campus of the university. As I've grown up, gigging in Aberystwyth has grown up with me.

Down the years I've had lots of adventures in the town – catching the last of a summer sunset over the sea after a hot and sticky train journey; me and the other comics fighting our way back to our digs in stupendous, knock-you-off-your-feet wind; a regrettable night at the end-of-days nightclub on the pier. From where I am now I can see that running has gradually supplanted drinking as the jumping-off point for these larks, and that this, of course, is probably for the best.

I was playing the Arts Centre on a Thursday, and I arranged a late checkout on the Friday so I could get a run in before driving across to Chester for my next show. But this was a B&B, not a big chain hotel, so late check-out meant 11 a.m. rather than 2 p.m. I got up sharp – the sun was shining – and joined the other comedians for breakfast; they had to catch an early train. So there we all were, at 7 a.m., none of us hungover, me eschewing food and sticking to black coffee. How times had changed. I remember one of those self-same comedians being with me in Aberystwyth years before, missing breakfast and then, when we phoned from the rainy promenade below his bedroom window to wake him up, flipping the finger at us, and flashing his arse for good measure. Of course, though clothed, we were in a similarly grubby state, like a beachfront *Withnail & I*.

Now I was up sharp, hoping to run half a marathon in preparation for two marathons that – little did I know then – would both be cancelled in the face of a global pandemic.

I'd worked out that if I ran north through the village of Borth and beyond, I'd reach a point that, according to my phone, was around six miles away by road. If I headed there and back via the coast path, that should come out at about half a marathon; six miles twice, plus country-side shenanigans: 13.1 miles. I'd be able to start with some healthful hill work as I zigzagged up across the funicular railway to the bluff that overlooks the town, and there was no chance of me going further than I wanted to, because beyond the apex of my planned run a broad channel stretched inland. If I got to Aberdovey, I would not only have gone further than I'd planned, I would also have done some impressive swimming.

While I'd been drinking coffee, the day's five minutes of sunshine had finished and it had begun to rain. I headed out into it, glancing at the beautiful breakers before plodding up to the rocky peak at the north end of the beach. Beyond the top, the wide, gravelled coast path was perfect for running, descending steadily to the deserted seaside arrangements of Borth – a nice cruise down, as long as I didn't think too hard about having to slog back up it on the return journey. Beyond the rainswept ice cream signs along the front of the winter-shuttered next-bay-along, the path narrowed, still clearly well used but no longer suited to Sunday afternoon push-chair strolls from one Cornetto outlet to the next. As the weather worsened, I reached a slightly precipitous stretch, where, although the path was good and there was heath-land grass and bracken dropping away to my left, it really *was* dropping away – steeply. My way was narrow and a bit slippery; it was some distance to the cliff-edge, let alone the sea, but a good slip and a cartoon cartwheel would get me there in an instant. I trod carefully.

The path – now feeling far more lonely and bleak than that misleading early stretch, but totally beautiful – became a patchwork of different surfaces to be approached with care: stony stretches were OK but could be treacherous; puddles I could run straight through, squelchy and chilly though that would be; grassy stretches were like ice rinks. But I was enjoying all this – I was ready for it. The wind blew the rain in hard from the north-west but I was warm enough, my cap kept it out of my eyes and I could feel it blowing satisfyingly across my open mouth. I dropped past a couple of stone buildings and crossed a stream before starting to climb again. The buildings laughed at the relative desertedness of the seaside spot I'd passed – 'No one back there till summer?' they seemed to say. 'Well, no one has *ever* been here and they *never will*!'

Perhaps I was tiring a little.

But I hadn't fallen over yet. I'd slipped and put a hand down on the slick, cold, sodden grass, but that doesn't count. And, as is always the case, my music was chivvying me up and driving me on. I climbed gently across a field – the smooth greenness of which belied the sudden rocky drop at its edge – then zigzagged through some gorse bushes before the path headed straight up the ridge of a conical hill – a little green mountain, to my eyes.

I didn't doubt coming out, or the route I had chosen, but I began to admit to myself that this was a serious run, in ways beyond miles on the map. And deep down I knew that I wasn't anywhere near my turning-back point. I plodded on.

Seeming to know exactly where I was at, my phone,

which I was beginning to think might need to be in a bowl of uncooked rice by the end of the day, played 'Gollum's Song', the piece that Emilíana Torrini – Icelandic but, no, she isn't Björk – sings over the end titles of *The Lord of the Rings: The Two Towers*. Such a deep, dark song, with soaring strings, sinister melodies and bowel-deep bass notes creating a doom-laden space around its lyrics of betrayal and lost hope. It hasn't got any pumping beats, but it's good running music, combining the personal-montage-sequence power of a huge orchestral film score with the images it conjures of climbing insurmountable, fantastical, jagged summits.

To me, a mountain is the quintessential metaphor for ambition and achievement. Climbing a mountain is always further, and often harder, than one's imagination can compass. The hazardous heights offer a vertiginous, dangerous perspective far beyond the day-to-day experience of modern life, and when you make it to the top, you can't fail to be amazed by what you've achieved. I dream of mountains when my working life is offering up exciting new challenges – and I seek out real-life mountains to climb in my time off. I'd visualised misty, fantastical mountains to carry on up in my earliest days of running, to take my mind off my struggle – and my treadmill – even as I began to feel light-headed from my then-unprecedented five-minute efforts. Now, here I was, very nearly living that, soundtrack and all – though it wasn't a mountain, I reminded myself, and there is very little that's filmic about being sodden. As the singing finished and the piece of music changed gear into its rousing, far more positive coda – the theme Howard Shore uses for Théoden King and the Horse Lords of Rohan, which has no lyrics but nevertheless sounds like 'this is a bit with horses in' – I reached the top of the little climb and also got over myself. My bamboo shorts were a mistake. They were trying their best to take in all the rainwater of Wales, and as a result were as heavy as can be and no longer staying up, a situation exacerbated by my near-total lack of buttocks.

The downhill beyond the mini mountain was all long grass, and running down it without falling involved a crazy string of slips, hops and jerks, my arms unhelpfully echoing the movements of my feet and legs in a kind of jazzy semaphore. This stretch was immediately followed by a steep path down to a bay – a path that had been helpfully equipped with those wooden steps good people build into muddy slopes. Each step held a deep puddle; I splashed down high-kicking, jazz hands and all, like a speeded-up coming-down-the-stairs sequence in a production of *Singin' in the Rain*. I comforted myself with the thought that I was the only person foolish enough to be out there, but this thought was rapidly followed by a daydream where I slipped off the cliff and, some time later, this moment of desperate showbiz was misinterpreted as me ending it all. I imagined myself, mid-fall, scrawling 'Don't worry guys – accident'. Because beyond this flight of steps, way below me, white waves crashed and black cliffs were now perfectly evident – and very unfriendly looking. There was one slab of rock directly below me; then, as I dropped back away from the brink, a small cove and another glowering cliff under a dark, stone obelisk. It really was more *Lord of the Rings* than Bognor Regis.

I ran on.

The obelisk, on a broad, grassy top, was a war memorial – not a pre-emptive Rob memorial, I was selfishly relieved to find. Beyond it, the high country dropped once again to holiday homes and then the sea. But instead of following my planned route down there, I took the hint, admitted a modicum of defeat, and turned for home.

It hadn't got any drier, flatter or easier, but the wind, when it got up, was at my back now. I was splashing up all those steps, but that meant I couldn't see the abyss below, and although I was carrying bamboo saddlebags of unnecessary water, I'd got to the point where I couldn't get any wetter. I'd got through the outward route without stopping or falling over. I could do this.

My goodness, what a soul-blast of a run. It was . . . extreme! Along those clifftops on the way back I saw birds – a big healthy kestrel, something gull-ish but unusual, maybe a kittiwake – enjoying the wind and I knew it was their day, not mine. I was a silly wet sod from London, out of my depth – nearly. Closing in on the civilisation I hadn't seen for what seemed like hours and hours, I slipped a little left, and, compensating, right, and, flailing to stay upright, had a moment thinking I'd be cartwheeling off the cliff after all, but – plot-spoiler – I made it back to Aberystwyth safe and sound.

I had run just over nine miles and been out for a little over two hours, but it felt . . . more. Some small part of me will always be out there, hoiking my shorts up and splashing along as the seabirds wheel below me. And perhaps I overstate the drama, but when I got back to the B&B – as the owners watched me, and the clock, carefully until I left – I told them where I'd been. 'Oh, is that path open again?' they said; 'It was closed for ages after that stretch of it slid into the sea . . .'

Another tune like this: Björk-esque high drama from a film soundtrack? Try Björk's own collaboration with David Arnold, 'Play Dead', from *The Young Americans* – a somewhat-forgotten nineties classic. I heard that, too, on the run in Aberystwyth.

Another run like this: The precipitous but fantastically well-kept paths above Lynmouth in Devon are wonderful, connecting the high cliffs of Countisbury to County Gate, the gorgeous white rapids of Watersmeet, Summerhouse Hill and on – over the hills or along the riverbanks – to the heights of Exmoor.

26. COMING UP

Clissold Park 2008 and De Beauvoir Town 2020

Looking back to those first weeks in September 2008, when I started running regularly, I envy myself experiencing it all for the first time. But it wasn't easy.

I was very much on the same page as all the people who've taken on the Couch to 5k challenge during the Covid-19 pandemic. What those runners don't realise – what *I* didn't realise – is that those first steps, stretching out a few minutes of effort to make it into something, then something more: they're the hardest part. When you're doing them, you can't imagine what it would be like to run far, to run regularly, to run without stopping – the magnitude of that effort is incomprehensible to the new runner. The truth is, the biggest thing of all is making those first forays; asking your body to do this stuff from a literal and metaphorical standing start.

It's the same when you first set out to become a comedian. Scratching together five to ten minutes of stuff to say, with no way to guarantee that you're going to say it in a funny way, then delivering it in some suboptimal scenario, like a lairy *Gong Show*, where the crowd are encouraged to boo you off, or some ill-equipped pub function room with a dozen unconvinced punters, or even a lovely, classy comedy club full of happy folk but where the compere has just teed you up by telling the audience to 'be kind – it's their first time' . . . All these gigs are so tough, but when you're going through them you think, 'If *this* is tough, what would it be like to close the show? To play to a thousand people? To be on stage for an hour?' The answer you can't possibly know at the time is: easier. Easier than this.

I remember running up the slight incline on the east side of Clissold Park, over two miles into one of those first three-milers – just a bit further on from where I heard Bon Iver, way back at the beginning of this book – and feeling the work my hips were doing to get me up that little slope. I visualised it – two discs of discomfort, grinding back and forth, like a rusty RoboCop – but here's the thing: it was a happy feeling, because I was so proud of myself for feeling it and running on.

It was also the beginning of a journey of discovery in terms of songs. I have always loved music – lived it, needed it, something which I share with my late, great dad. I've always had very catholic taste, but in my late teens I fought that instinct to some extent, developing a predictable snootiness about some genres and bands because they weren't cool or because they wore their heart on their sleeve. So Dad's mature, and maturing, music choices bewildered me. I really respected his taste and perspective, and he won round my teen ego by listening to, and often liking, the tapes I left in his car – but how could he listen to, say, country and western?!

I'm not saying I like all music these days – and though my dad tried, I don't believe he ever enjoyed any of the techno with a screaming Roland 303 bass sequencer on it that I left in his car stereo – but I think both of us found new ways to enjoy music long after we were teenagers. Maybe for him this was enhanced by, and in turn enhanced, his daily commute in the company of his car's cassette deck. For me, it was running that brought me back. I had reached a point in life where I rarely thought to put in headphones, and my music collection – only just moving from CDs to a PC-based playlist back in the noughties – simply didn't need to comprise more than a bunch of long-loved albums.

Once I started running I suddenly needed a playlist that was entirely made up of stone-cold classics – diverse and extensive enough to be able to surprise me. By necessity, I cast my net a little wider; once the music I already knew I loved was on there, I added things that challenged me: new music, stuff I had loved but hadn't heard for years, film soundtracks, and tunes that were simply challenging in terms of sound – the kind of thing that would frighten the kids if you played it in the living room.

Plus – yes – I got less snooty.

When U2 took over the musical world in the eighties – from Live Aid to *The Joshua Tree* – my friends and I couldn't stand them. Bono's posturing, their love for Americana, the fact that they were almost a *rock* band! All this felt distasteful to us. And although I understood them better and respected them more as I got older, I wouldn't ever have sought them out to listen to if it wasn't for running. But I heard 'Vertigo' playing that September, admitted to myself it was great, and stuck it on my silly little clip-music-player.

I could see by then that, as an Irish band, their relationship with America was different to that of, say, the Smiths, and that the Americana of *The Joshua Tree* is a choice – an artistic exploration of that relationship. By 2008 I got that the Edge is very much a new-wave guitarist who was as eager, in the eighties, to shun the blues-based clichés and screaming solos of Led Zeppelin and AC/DC as I would have been, and that the crunching, power-chord riff on 'Vertigo' is him letting himself try out their musical language in a way that he'd avoided up to that point.

Now, thanks to running, I understood more than ever that none of that matters.

How does a song sound after a couple of miles – or more? Is it welcome? Will it help? These are the only important questions.

I had breezed into Clissold Park that September in 2008 forgetting to be tired or to even worry about running, because I was caught up in the counterintuitive autumnal sadness of that Bon Iver track. I had pushed on up the other side of the park on my RoboCop hips and completed a circuit. Now I turned to cross the park on the diagonal – a great path pointing up through the green to Clissold House, the skyscraping steeple of the church behind it and, beyond them, home.

It's another incline, but that didn't figure. I just thought, *I will keep running – as fast as I can – up here and onward to my front door, and only then will I stop*. 'Vertigo' began – driving drums, the Edge's strummed, dampened strings, Bono saying 'One, two, three, fourteen!' in Spanish, then that riff, so rocky it's more suited to air guitar than the real thing. It was welcome. It helped. No cyborg plod for me this time; I ran like I was in a movie, and as I reached the heart of the park, at the top of the slope, in the middle of the song, I felt a great, physical rush as my body hit me up with all the chemicals I needed. A prickling wave rolled up the back of my head from the nape of my neck to the top, and I chuckled – a pure, observable, physical high – from running, and listening, to – of all bands – U2! Who knew?!

This was running, I thought. These were the endorphins I'd heard tell of. From here on in, I expected to feel this way often. But it wasn't to be. Every time you push your body, it learns. It resets what it will happily do for you, based on what you ask of it. So the next time I ran fast through the heart of Clissold Park at the end of a run, there were no naturally secreted intoxicants for me. 'You've got this,' my system seemed to say, unconcerned, and left me to get home on my own.

Like a shark, a runner needs to keep moving forward or die – or stop being a runner, at least. This is as true in a single run as it is in life. We're always chasing, trying to get to that next mile-marker, that next achievement, that next target – not just because we're addicted to the game, but because everything we make our body achieve, it immediately takes for granted. 'Done that. What do you want from me next?' So, before too long I could look back on that innocent, achy-hipped high brought on by U2 at around two and a half miles as a sweet memory, a place I couldn't – wouldn't – go back to. My tri-weekly runs climbed to seven miles, I did a half marathon, a marathon, I started going to parkruns, 10k races . . . the whole deal. And my playlist, though always carefully curated, became incredibly diverse – and damn near infinite.

Twelve years later, everything about 2008 seems like it's from another life – and not just in terms of running.

And yet . . .

This week I ran to Victoria Park, around it, and home. Maybe because I've been telling you all these tales of running fast from a time when I didn't know any other way, I set off down the hill from Newington Green at a fiercer pace than I usually would these days, and I maintained it.

The nature of algorithms, and chances being what they are, my phone played me song after song from those I've written about here in *Running Tracks* – and they all still sounded great. Sprinkled between them were newer, wilder discoveries – the Day-Glo, computer-game-sounding rock-with-sixties-girl-group-vocals of Crying's 'Wool in the Wash' from their album *Beyond the Fleeting Gales*, a record celebrated in comedian James Acaster's 2016-was-the-best-year-ever-for-music book *Perfect Sound Whatever*; the hard, spooky bass and beats, entirely vocal- and instrument-free, of Daniel Avery's mighty 'Diminuendo'; and, from the Disney film *Zootropolis,* which we watched as a family the other day, nostalgically, as those little children are big teenagers now, Shakira's 'Try Everything' – cheesy, poppy, on-the-nose, and absolutely wonderful.

The only thing better than running while listening to music is running *fast* while listening to music. As Shakira's distinctively sung, compellingly syncopated hymn to openness and experimentation – a joyous exhortation to risk failure if you want to experience the highest heights of life – played, I had a little cry and turned right into the last mile home, up a pretty street in De Beauvoir Town that I must have run along thirty, forty times this summer alone.

And as the chorus caught on my heart, and I laboured to keep going as fast as I had been, a prickling wave rolled up the back of my head, from the nape of my neck to the top, and I chuckled; maybe if you go a bit too fast, for a bit too long, and run up a little hill to an upbeat, poppy song, a natural high is always available after all.

Another tune like this: 'Sugar Rush', the J-Pop wonder from the end titles of *Wreck-It Ralph*.

Another run like this: Any run that finishes with that slight hill not far from your house – but make sure you take it at a bit of a lick.

26.2

That's what it's like for me to go running with a bit of music in my headphones, and I hope you can see how absolutely defining and important it is for me – and how personal. There are as many ways to run, physically and mentally, as there are runners, but only some of those ways involve headphones, and even fewer involve music. Some people love the company of a great podcast; still more, I'm sure, don't need either – just the sounds of the world – to find their perfect running space.

What I've realised, telling you these stories, is what an important part of my running story marathons have become. I'm a marathon runner! I really hadn't noticed. That was never my plan, and it still feels like Somebody Else's Thing, but here we are, at the end of a decade where I've run fourteen of the things. How did that happen? I suppose it's partly because, naturally, I'm a distance runner; I gravitated very quickly to running for an hour – six, seven miles – when others in my shoes might have worked for months to run ten kilometres and then felt most at home at a parkrun, perfecting their five. That's right – straight from miles to kilometres without a word of warning. Stay with me.

But on another level, marathon running – British marathon running, in particular, it would seem – is about fundraising. Not just fundraising, but the opportunity that fundraising presents for processing trauma, tragedy, sadness and loss. Taking the worst, most pressing issues of one's life and, through extreme challenge, alchemising them into joy. And cash.

So I've taken to running as far as I possibly can – and then going five, six miles further. And I've justified that quest to myself – all that time, training and solitude I've put in – by raising money for Parkinson's UK, the charity wrestling with the condition that slowly but surely took my dad away from me. Plus, I've found all manner of friends, stories and other, non-running-related adventures along the way. I'm really glad I did.

So there are twenty-six stories here, one for each full mile of a marathon. All that's left now is the point-two. Finally, the all-important little detail that brings me home – beyond the headphones and, I suppose, the running, let alone all that real-life stuff – is my relationship with music. I don't just listen to other people's songs, I write my own, and spending time with music is something I was doing for thirty years before I took even my first trot. And just as I wouldn't hector a runner who does it without music to change their ways, neither would I tell you what songs you should be listening to out there.

But I do wonder what works best.

If I was to try to write the perfect running tune – which I am – what would I need? Repetitive beats, of course, to echo and celebrate the pulse of your heart, the power of your lungs, the rhythm of your legs, but more than that – for their rattling, galvanising relentlessness; they're going to keep on coming, so you can keep on going.

Not just beats – bass. Deep and visceral, picked or processed, the low grooves that will get you right in the gut and, again, keep you rolling along – unless the effect on your gut is too real and you have to stop; happens to the best of us.

Which brings us to squelchy, synthesiser blasts that grow up out of those basslines, taking that dance music into the anthemic arena of choruses, without losing the pulse. And also, in a higher register, soaring synths – or strings – or vocals – the angelic-chorus chords that create the sky that arches over the ground, even as you pound it down below.

Of course, we don't only need electronics. There will have to be guitars – crunchy, long-haired rock riffs to make you feel like you're on a motorbike; lyrics, and vocal performances, that chime with your experience while simultaneously lifting you out of it. And not songs about running, but songs – or just words or phrases – about travelling, dreaming, moving, dancing; songs of hope and joy but tinged with sadness, effort, loss – the battle of life. Samples, too, not just singing, with clips and blips to soundtrack the movie that is your run.

And for every huge dance banger or raging metal thrash, a pensively strummed acoustic guitar ballad; for every hands-in-the-air crescendo, a spooky, empty moment of quiet.

Some musical yin for every yang.

Shouldn't be too hard . . . but it might need to be more than one song.

Will I succeed in making new music to match the tracks in this book that have meant so much to me? Well, I'll write something, and put it on my playlist, and maybe one day – on a hillside, towpath, finish line, treadmill – I'll hear it start and my paces will lengthen, my body will straighten, my eyes will lift to the horizon, and I'll think . . . *Yes!*

ACKNOWLEDGEMENTS

It's gratifying to know that the names of all the people who brought this book into existence are printed here; thank you so much. At the risk of stating the obvious, without you this would not have been possible.

Thank you too to everyone who has sponsored me in running events for Parkinson's UK down the years – you've given them thousands and thousands of pounds. There's a lot of crossover between those two groups, which just goes to show what a special, supportive, generous bunch of people you all are. The third circle in this Venn diagram of kindness is the *Running Commentary* community, who are so free with their love for each other and us. Thank you, marshals.

I'm sure Paul T would agree, it's a level of positivity we're not used to after the cynicism of the stand-up comedy scene – but hey, that's fun too. I want to thank the Comedy Store, the Stand, the Glee Club, Komedia and Little Wander for making so many of these runs possible, and providing lovely, lovely gigs to go with them. And thank you to Parkinson's UK not just for the marathon and half marathon places around the world they've provided for me, but also for the comedy nights and the TV quizzes; years of fun and adventures.

Thank you, incredible running event organisers: Parkrun, RunThrough, Great Run, It's Grim Up North Running, Royal Parks Half, Bath Half, the London Marathon and the Yorkshire Marathon.

Thank you to Unbound themselves for facilitating this project, in particular Katy Guest for her belief in me, DeAndra Lupu for her patience with me, and Mecob for bringing my design dreams to life so stylishly.

Thanks to Steve Campen, who makes the *Running Commentary* podcast possible – with skill and charm – and to Paul Tonkinson, who makes it wonderful, worthwhile and wise, despite being . . . a little foolish. And what a runner! Thanks for the inspiration, Tonks, and the silly voices.

Thanks to Steve Lamacq, not just for making some of the most exciting running here possible, but also for consistently wanting to hear me talk about music. Thanks to the other legends who appear in these pages: Lauren Laverne, the mighty Susie Chan, Mickey D, Barry Castagnola, the ever-ebullient Tony Audenshaw and the band Public Service Broadcasting who – along with featuring heavily – helped spread the word.

Thanks to Sarah and Richard, Trapper and Mo and Nigel and Trish for providing the heavenly homes away

ACKNOWLEDGEMENTS

from home behind some of the most dramatic scenery in these pages.

Thanks to my mum and dad for their love and support, and special mention to Mum for taking care of Dad through the toughest times.

And thank you to Julia, Buddy and Daisy, always there cheering me on, at mile seventeen and throughout life. None of this means anything without you. You brought sweets.

A NOTE ON THE AUTHOR

Rob Deering is a writer, comedian, broadcaster, musician and theatre director. He spent the 1990s writing music and directing plays before becoming a stand-up comedian at the turn of the century. Since then he has become one of the UK's most in-demand comedy headliners, toured the world and taken nine solo shows to the Edinburgh Festival Fringe. Over time Rob brought music back into his comedy, adding guitars, pedals and vocals to his stand-up act and becoming a twenty-first-century one-man band. He created Parkinson's UK's successful Shake with Laughter comedy nights – with those, the many marathons and several TV quizzes, he's raised over £125k for the charity.

In recent years he has also returned to directing – comedians this time. He's a regular on BBC Radio 6 Music and one of the hosts of the *Comedy Club* on BBC Radio 4 Extra. He records the popular *Running Commentary* podcast whilst running with fellow comedian Paul Tonkinson.

He lives with his wife and children in North London.

INDEX

Unbound is the world's first crowdfunding publisher, established in 2011.

We believe that wonderful things can happen when you clear a path for people who share a passion. That's why we've built a platform that brings together readers and authors to crowdfund books they believe in – and give fresh ideas that don't fit the traditional mould the chance they deserve.

This book is in your hands because readers made it possible. Everyone who pledged their support is listed below. Join them by visiting unbound.com and supporting a book today.

THANK YOU

Every item you buy or donate
helps beat poverty.

We offer a 30-day refund policy for items returned to store in the
condition they were sold in, with proof of purchase and with valid
price ticket attached to the item. View full T&Cs in-store or at
www.oxfam.org.uk/high-street-faqs

Join our team and help
beat poverty for good

www.oxfam.org.uk/volunteer

THANK YOU

Every item you buy or donate
helps beat poverty.

We offer a 30-day refund policy for items returned to store in the
condition they were sold in, with proof of purchase and with valid

OXFAM

VAT: 348 4542 38

Volunteer here: Have fun,
meet new people & learn
new skills
Sign up in-store or at
www.oxfam.org.uk/jointheteam

| REBECCA | SALES | F4625/POS1 |

FRIDAY 15 OCTOBER 2021   13:44 044397

| 1 | C5 - HOBBIES | £4.00 |

1 Items

| TOTAL | **£4.00** |
| CREDIT CARD | £4.00 |

Oxfam Shop: F4625
45, Heath Street
Hampstead, London, NW3 6UA
02077943060
oxfam.org.uk/shop

Lynn Birchall
Alex Blackall
David Blackman
Judi Bond
Kevin Bonfield
Magdalena Boo
Anne-Marie Booth
Rich Booth
Timothy Borg
Kirsty Bradshaw
Martin Branney
Dave Brett
Jen Brister
Alex Brodie
Kristian Brodie
Rod Brookes
Brian Broughton
Mark Brown
Brian Browne
Simon Burcham
James Burdett
Ali Burns
Phil Cairns
Sophie Cameron
Paul Camp
Gavin Campbell
Davey Candlish
Oliver Cannon
Drummond Cargill
Catherine Carlin
Helen Carrick
Claire Carroll

Steve Carson
Damon Carter
John-Jo Carter
Rob Carthy
Simon Cartlidge
Rebecca Cartwright-
    Teakle
Seth Cayley
Gary Chape
Chris Checkley
Matt Chester
David Christie
Jarred "Shut Up
    Body" Christmas
Martin Clark
Neil Clark
Ellie Clarke
Rob Clarke
Rose Clarke
Gemma Cloney
Adam Clothier
Allison Coggan
Tricia Coleman
Kate Collins
Lisa Condron
Simon Connelly
Richard Conroy
Scott Conroy
Liam Cook
Richard Cook
Barry & Julie Cooper
Ben Cooper

Jason Cope
Matthew Cormack
David Cornock
Jonathan Coulthard
Steven Cowan
David Crawford
Jane Crawford
Toby Crick
Gareth Crook
Keith Cruickshank
Peter Cummings
Christopher John
    Cunningham
Matt Cuthbert
D.B.Parsons
John Daly
Chris Daniels
Tom Dark
Eileen Davidson
Barbara M Deering
Adam Dempsey
Paul Denman
Jeremy Denton
The Development
    Team Unbound
Liz Dexter
Paul Dickin
Angela Dickson
Debbie Dillon
Frances Dillon
Deirdre Dobson
Ian Dodds

James Dodsworth
Alice Doggrell
Judith Doherty
Ben Dorkins
Lynne Doyle
Juanita Draude
Simon Dring
Rhian Drinkwater
Simon Duck
Davie Duncan
Adrienne Dunkerley
Allison Dunne
Luke Dunwoody
Will Dupre
Mair Dyer
Rob Dyer
Dave Eagle
John Eastwood
Tony Edgar
Paul Edmonds
Adam Edwards
Christine Edwards
Peter Edwards
Katherine Ellis
Paul Ellis
Tom Ellis
Tracey Emery
Brioney Euden
David Evans
Michael Evans
Rob Evans
Sally Evans

Laura Everitt
Johnny Eveson
Michael Ewing
Lauren Farmer
Sarah Faust
James Featherstone
Michael Fenwick
Jacqui Ferris
Jo Fielding
Nate Filer
Carl Finch
Ian Finch
Simon Finch
Kieron Finlay
Fiona Finlayson
Michelle Flower
Agnes Flues
Colin Forbes
Helen Ford
Rob Ford
Teresa Forgione
Alastair Forrester
Steven Fowler
Nicky Foy
Andy Freeman
Paul Frost
Cat Fursman
Steven Gadd
Tanith Galer
Steven Gallagher
Chris Gardner
Matthew Garner

Ann Gash
Eian Gault
Carly Gear
Ian Geddes
Dan Gelder
Tom George
Simon Gerhardt
Anna Gibson
Thomas Gibson
Julie Giles
Simon Giles
Jason Good
Ruth Goodchild
Simon Gosney
Jeremy Graham
Richard Gray
Steve Gray
John Greehy
Andrew Green
James Greveson
    Hickie
Tracey Griffiths
Laura Grimshaw
Pia Groenewolt
Katy Guest
Chris Guy
Eleanor Haig
Garry Haining
Clive Hall
Ian T Hall
Lisa Hall
The Halls

SUPPORTERS

Nicki Hamilton
Maria Harrington
Lee Harris
Claire Hart
Mark Hart
Sarah Hayes
Mel Heale
Joe Heap
Catherine Herbert
Graham Hewitt
Clair Hibbert
Sandra Higgison
David Hill
Rich Hill
Rob Hill
Beverley Hilton
Darren Hilton
Louise Hobson
David Hodges
Gemma Holden
John Holland
Neil Holland
Fran Hollinrake
Chris Holmes
Darren Hooley
Graeme Horstead
Ian Hoskins
Dan Houghton
Michael Hoult
Richard Howard
Robert Hudson
Ben Hughes

David Hughes
Rona Hunnisett
Dale Hunt
Roz Hunter
Kevin Hutchings
Martin Hutchinson
Lee Innes
David Irwin
Helen Iveson
Oliver Ivory-Bray
Maureen Jackson
Paul Jackson-Clark
Andrew Jacobs
Emma James
Sarah James
Joseph Jameson
Paul Jamieson
David Jarvis
Jemma Jarvis
Ivan Jeary
Rob Jesson
Kirsten Johnson
Mark Johnson
Helen Johnston
Rachel Johnston
Steve Jones
Suzi Jones
Kathryn Joy
John Keane
Julie Kearney
Simon Kelly
Sophie Kelsall

Rich Kemp
Pam Kennedy
Kevin's Imaginary
    Friend
Amjid Khan
Sarah U Khan
Dan Kieran
David King
Sam Knibbs
Audrey Laidlaw
Megan Lamb
Jason Lamont
Mike Lane
Matt Larkin
Chris Last
Andy Latham
Rachael Leary-Wood
Hania Lee
Tony Lee
Phil Lengthorn
Matt Lewis
Sophie Lewis
Tom Lewis
Laura Lexx
Benjamin Light
Adam Little
Jonathan Russell
    Lloyd
Wilma Lock
Ali Lockett
Sean Loddick
Alan Lord

Philippa Lord
Simon Lynch
Jaclyn M
Gary MacAlister
Emily Macaulay
Edith MacLean
Malcolm MacLean
Mark MacLean
Angus MacLeod
Jessica Maier
Catherine Makin
Dale Maltby
Daniel Marks
Paul Marley
Louise Marshall
Ness Marshall
Stacey Marston
Ian Martin
Lenny Martin
Mason family
Paul Mathew
Amy Matthews
Ian Maullin
Tom Mayhew
A McAllister
Rachel McCann
Freegas Mccheese
Nigel McConachie
David McCormick
Terry McDermott
Alan McDougall
Catherine McGarr

James McGeehan
Patrick McHugh
Samuel Mcilwaine
Colleen McKenna
Gavin McKeown
Louise McLaren
Michael McLaughlin
Andrew McLennan
Iain McNicol
Stuart McNicol
Joe McVey
Louisa Mead
Kirsty Medlock
Simon Mehigan
Matthew Melksham
Matthew Michael
Ally Middleton
Alex Miell
Scott Millar
Colin Miller
Keith Miller
David Miskin &
    Tom Appleby
Andrew Mitchell
James Mitchell
Kay Mitchell
John Mitchinson
Alan Mochrie
Ben Moffat
Willie Moffat
Mark Momola
Tony Mooney

Emma Miranda
    Moore
Ben Moorhouse
Craig Moran
Martin Morgan
Stuart Morgan
Mark Morgan-
    Hillam
Alex Morris
Keith Morris
Philip Morris
Jim Moyle
@mr_spoon
Todd Mundle
Terry Murray
David Mutters
Rosalba Napolitano
Helen Nash
Carlo Navato
Laura Neale
Colin Neilson
David Nelson
John Nichol
Nigel
Chris Norman
Gerard Nugent
Sarah Nye
Brendan O'Donovan
Sharon O'Leary
Robin O'Neill
Sean O'Sullivan
Stephen O'Shea

SUPPORTERS

Matt Olczak
Jenny Oldridge
Licinio Oliveira
Gordon Orr
Neil Park
Frances Parsons
Luke Partridge
Stewart Paterson
Nick Patrick
David Payne
Gareth Payne
Sam Payne
Lara Peach
Catherine Penketh
Hannah Persson
Janice Phayre
Richard Phillips
Seb Philpott
Juliette Pichat
Nick Pidgeon
Kenny Pieper
Madeline Pilbury
Matt Pitcher
Matthew Poade
Matthew James
    Poade
Justin Pollard
Lucy Porter
Alistair Potter
Jean Power
Richard Prangle
Chris Pratt

Tom Price
Jane Probett
Kirsten Proctor
Charlotte Proud
Andrus Purde
Joe Pymont
Gary Qualter
Queen Jane the Great
Sally Quinn
Duncan Raggett
Aseem Rahman
John Rainsforth
David Ratcliffe
Phillip Ratcliffe
Steven Rawlins
Paul Readman
Simon Reap
Simon Reeve
Nick Rennie
Clare Richardson
Joe Richardson
Paula Richardson
Sally & Ed Ripley
Piero Rizzi
Julian Roberts
Nick Robinson
Peter Robinson
Jon Rodgers
Antony Rose
Gillian Ross
Leon Ross
Phil Rowlands

Richard Rowling
Sarah Roy
Lisa Rull
Jon Rumley
Louise S
John Salisbury
Adrian Saunders
Jeni Sawford
Colin Saxon
Carol Sayles
Johannes Schneider
Liza SD
Heather Shannon
Jonathan Sharp
Kevin Sheahan
Rick Sherman
Richard Shilton
Ian Shurmer
Rachel Simmonite
Dave Singleton
Helen Singleton
Ian Smith
Kevin Smith
Sally Smith
Lee South
Ian Squire
Brett Srawley
Wendy Staden
Mimi Steer
Darren Stockdale
Jenny Stones
Stewart Strath

Paul Summerhill

Marcus Sweeney-Bird

Philip T Symeonides

Clare Taalab

Phillip Tailby

Baz Taylor

Chris Taylor

Genevieve Taylor

Gerry Taylor

Graham Taylor

Jonathan JT Taylor

Tell you I chose

Mark Terris

Pete Thacker

Deri Thomas

Hannah Thomas

Sarah Thompson

Simon Thompson

Sarah Thorndyke

Amabel Thornton

Andrew Thornton

Sophie Thurman

Eleanor Tiernan

Laurence Timms

Lee Todd

James Tombs

Paul Tonkinson

Marcus Toombs

Jamie Townsend

Craig Tripney

Alison Trott

Jonathan Tucker

Clive Tulloh

Andrew Tunnicliffe

Susan Turnbull

Michael Twine

Helen Urquhart

Bas van Kaam

Keith Vance

Ivan Wainewright

Hayley Waldron

Chris Wales

Emma Walker

Stacey Wall

Colin (Wally)Wallace

Jamie Ward

Katherine Ward

Robert Warman

Matthew Warr

Paula Warrington

Andrew Watkins

Mark Watson

Sally Watson

Andy Watt

Tam Weaver

Chris West

Kimberley West

Christopher Westcott

Anita Westmorland

Alun Westoll

Sam Whalley

Vicky Wheatley

Nick White

Stephen Wicks

Neil Wightman

David Wilding

Nicky Wilkinson

Paul Willgoss MBE

Allan Williams

Graham Williams

Jeni Williams

James Willis

Derek Wilson

Ruth Wilson

Julia Winborn

Andrew Wood

Michelle Woodcock

Matt Wooden

Alex Woods

Richard Woods

Zoe Woodward

Hayley Leanne Wragg

Dave Wright

Kate Wynne

Debbie Wythe

Anthony Yates

Susan Young

Imran Yusuf